The Structure of
Personal Characteristics

THE STRUCTURE OF PERSONAL CHARACTERISTICS

David M. Romney
and John M. Bynner

PRAEGER

Westport, Connecticut
London

Library of Congress Cataloging-in-Publication Data

Romney, David M.
    The structure of personal characteristics / David M. Romney and
John M. Bynner.
        p. cm.
    Includes bibliographical references and index.
    ISBN 0–275–93995–2 (alk. paper)
    1. Psychometrics. 2. Psychology—Statistical methods.
3. Ability—Research—Statistical methods. 4. Personality
disorders—Research—Statistical methods. 5. Self-perception—
Research—Statistical methods. 6. Path analysis. I. Bynner, John
M. II. Title.
    BF39.R545   1992
    155.2'3—dc20   92–18845

British Library Cataloguing in Publication Data is available.

Library of Congress Catalog Card Number: 92–18845
ISBN: 0–275–93995–2

First published in 1992

Praeger Publishers, 88 Post Road West, Westport, Connecticut 06881
An imprint of Greenwood Publishing Group, Inc.

Printed in the United States of America

The paper used in this book complies with the
Permanent Paper Standard issued by the National
Information Standards Organization (Z39.48–1984).

10 9 8 7 6 5 4 3 2 1

This book is dedicated to Karl Jöreskog for pioneering the field of structural equation modeling and for creating with Dag Sörbom the computer program LISREL.

Contents

Illustrations

TABLES

Preface

Omnis Fluit

—Heraclitus (537–425 B.C.)

How people perform on certain tasks, how they behave in various situations, and how they perceive and interpret the world, all depend to a large extent on their personal characteristics. Therefore, to understand individuals and to be able to make predictions about them, knowledge of their personal characteristics, that is, their abilities, traits, and attitudes, becomes of paramount importance. The traditional psychometric approach that has been used to explore personal characteristics is factor analysis (FA). However, this approach can provide only one type of model—the factor model—to explain the data. The factor model assumes that there are underlying latent variables or factors that are responsible for the intercorrelations among the variables. This type of model typically represents abilities, traits, and attitudes as static entities that are largely resistant to change. Consequently, the factor-analytic approach is regarded by many as sterile and leading to a dead end. The purpose of this book is to show that in all three domains there are alternative structural models to factor models, such as simplexes and circumplexes, which (1) fit the data better, (2) make more sense theoretically, (3) and have greater utility.

The routine fitting of the factor model to correlated data is not acceptable because the basic assumption made by the factor model that these variables must have a factor or factors in common may be wrong. For instance, two variables may be correlated because one gives rise to the other or because they affect each other reciprocally, and not because they are both measuring the same thing. This fundamental change in the way we look at relationships between psychological and social variables has fueled the growth of a field which has come to be known as structural-equation modeling (SEM), and has thereby encouraged the production of computer programs such as LISREL, EQS, and COSAN.

The advantages of this new approach are manifold. First, unlike in factor analysis, not all our eggs are placed in one basket because we can interpret correlations in more than one way. Second, we can derive and test theoretical models that contain hypotheses about how variables and factors may influence each other, that is, the directionality of causal influence. And third, we can compute estimates of the regression coefficient parameters that may reveal to us the size of the effect that changing one variable or factor might have on another, an important issue when a possible intervention is being considered. Thus, SEM is a much more comprehensive technique than FA because it allows us to examine path models as well as factor models for explaining the relationships between variables. In fact, SEM is a combination of factor analysis and path analysis, performing the functions of both and enabling us to test dynamic models which trace pathways between factors and to infer their causal relationships.

The advent of SEM has led to a number of reanalyses of correlational data collected in the various domains in order to gain the new insights which SEM can provide. Using this approach, we have investigated personal characteristics in three psychological domains—abilities, personality disorders, and self-attitudes—and have examined alternative models to the common-factor model to explain data that have been collected empirically. We summarize our achievements in these areas based on a series of studies that we have conducted over several years. The book concludes with a discussion of our findings from both theoretical and practical perspectives, that is, their implications for teaching, therapy, and communication. Finally, we point the way to new directions for research indicated by SEM, a treasure trove of possibilities.

ACKNOWLEDGMENTS

We are especially grateful to the University of Calgary for awarding David Romney a Killam Resident Fellowship for the fall term of 1991, which allowed him to devote more time to completing this book. We are also grateful to the British Council for awarding John Bynner a travel grant that enabled him to come to Calgary to work jointly on the book in the spring of 1991.

The data came from a variety of sources. We wish to acknowledge particularly the help of Dr. Phil Clift and the Great Barr School in Birmingham, England, where the ability test data were collected; Dr. Jerald Bachman and the Institute for Social Research at the University of Michigan where the Youth in Transition Study was conducted; and the U.K. Economic and Social Research Council that funded the 16–19 Initiative surveys.

Our thanks also go to Gary Willis, who edited the text; Maureen

Howard, who compiled the Author and Subject indexes; Sheila Young and Sharon Clarke in SSRU at City University, who did some of the typing; and Jacques Romney and Bohdan Bilan, who drew the original figures for the book. Finally, we wish to thank our wives, Claude and Val, for putting up with our obsession and giving us their continuing support.

The Structure of
Personal Characteristics

Chapter 1

Exploration and Confirmation

WHAT ARE PERSONAL CHARACTERISTICS?

How people perform on cognitive tasks, how they behave in various situations, and how they perceive and interpret the world and what they feel about it, all depend to a large extent on their personal characteristics. The fact that people differ from each other on these characteristics attests to their individuality and uniqueness. One way that people differ is in their specific *abilities*. Some people are better than others with words (verbal ability) or with numbers (numerical ability), and some are better at practical skills where they need to use their hands (manual dexterity). The origins of these abilities are unclear. We may or may not be born with the potential to develop different types of ability. But as our knowledge of them comes through their manifestation in the performance of tasks, whatever is inherited in them is overlaid with learning and experience.

Differences in ability alone, however, are not enough to ensure success in life; in addition to ability there has to be the motivation and opportunity to succeed. Striving for success or the need to achieve is a personality trait and, like ability, is not distributed among us equally. Some individuals are ambitious, dominant, and competitive, whereas others may be just the opposite. It is the former who tend to have successful careers, because ability alone is not enough. Different kinds of traits are shown by people who are relaxed, sociable, and easy to get along with in contrast to those who are tense, shy, and withdrawn. Our personality is formed by a constellation of traits that dispose us to behave in a particular way over time in a variety of circumstances. But our behavior is also determined in part by our beliefs and by our attitudes towards ourselves, which may in turn be influenced by our values. If we believe, for instance, that our personal worth depends upon our success in life, then failure to realize our ambitions may lead to a loss of self-esteem and to feelings of depression. Thus abilities, traits, and attitudes play a key role in our lives. Let us, therefore, consider them more closely.

Because tests that measure specific abilities intercorrelate positively with each other (i.e., people who are good at one kind of activity also tend to be good at other kinds of activity), the British psychologist Charles Spearman (1927) inferred that a general factor, common to all the ability tests, is being measured as well. This general underlying factor, which Spearman called *g,* has been equated with intelligence. The American psychologist L. L. Thurstone (1947) challenged this view; he thought that the correlations between the tests should be explained in terms of "group" factors, such as "verbal ability," "numerical ability," and so on. The existence of conflicting views makes the point that concepts such as intelligence are *theoretical constructs* that cannot be measured directly but can only be inferred indirectly from one's performance on those tasks that are supposed to measure it. Consequently, we are never too sure what we mean by "intelligence," and we may have to define it operationally. Specific abilities are also theoretical constructs; however, this seems to be less of a problem because the tests that measure them have obvious content validity. For instance, a test measuring numerical ability will usually entail some computing, and a test of verbal ability will usually include vocabulary items.

   In the same way as there are many different abilities, there are many different personality traits. These latter are relatively enduring attributes that dispose us to respond in a particular way. They need to be differentiated from states that are transient expressions of moods and seem to be affected by the particular situation we happen to be in. An example of a trait would be meticulousness, which characterizes people who are extremely thorough, very neat and tidy in their habits, and who are so well organized that they never miss an appointment or forget a birthday and always arrive on time. Unlike tests assessing abilities, personality measures or scales do not all intercorrelate positively: In some cases there appears to be no relationship at all between them, and in others there is even a negative correlation between the two measures that correlate positively with a third. This latter finding is not surprising when one considers how different people are, and that some people seem to be almost the exact opposite of others as far as their personalities are concerned. Nevertheless, because of the "clustering" of some personality traits—some seem to occur together—it has been hypothesized that they can be reduced to a few common factors. One theory (Eysenck 1970) is that two general factors (later extended to three) are required to account for the matrix of correlations among scales measuring more specific personality traits. These two fundamental factors of personality are postulated to be *extroversion* and *neuroticism.* Extroverts are outgoing individuals who enjoy company and are the opposite of introverts; neurotics are anxious and highly strung compared with normal people. A third factor, *psychoticism,* was also postulated but received little attention in the personality literature. Three other important personality factors that have subsequently been claimed are *agreeableness, conscientiousness,* and *openness to experience.* These latter three factors, together with extroversion and neuroticism, are known as the Big Five dimensions of personality (Wiggins & Trapnell, in press), but again we must emphasize that this is just another theory about the structure of personality and should not be accepted as an incontrovertible fact.

There are virtually as many attitudes as there are people; there does not seem to be a limit to the topics about which people have an attitude. We gave self-attitude as an example, but there are attitudes to food, sex, television, jeans, mountain bikes, and so on. While most of us share many attitudes, some of us may have attitudes held by only a few people. Attitudes not only vary according to their content, they also differ in intensity; that is, they may be held strongly or weakly. Essentially an attitude is an evaluative belief, and hence it has been argued that there is a general factor of evaluation (good or bad) that underlies all attitudes and accounts largely for the correlations among them (Osgood, Suci, & Tannenbaum 1957). Others have constructed attitude hierarchies, with broad value dimensions at the top and more specific attitudes to issues such as the police and privatization further down (cf. Eysenck 1957b; Oppenheim 1966; Rokeach 1968).

MEASUREMENT OF PERSONAL CHARACTERISTICS

A host of tests and scales exist for measuring personal characteristics. These constitute the tools of the professional psychologist. Ability tests require that subjects do their best to get the right answer, often within a given time limit, whereas personality and attitude scales expect subjects to answer how they would behave or think *typically* in response to a particular situation. All psychological tests are plagued with problems of *reliability* and *validity,* some more than others. As with physical measurement, psychological measurement is not free from error. With physical measurement, however, we can measure an object several times and then take the average measurement as the true one, assuming of course that the errors in measurement occur at random and are, therefore, able to cancel each other out. This strategy is not feasible with psychological measurement because the subject's responses will be affected first (positively) by practice and later (negatively) by fatigue. Two solutions to the problem were developed by psychologists. From the correlations between measurements of the same test repeated at a suitably long interval, an estimate of the measurement error can be obtained. By splitting the test in two and determining the correlation between the two halves or by determining the correlation between all items in the test, another type of reliability estimate can be obtained. The former type of reliability is now usually referred to as *stability* and the latter as *internal consistency* (Cronbach 1970; Wheaton, Muthén, Alwin, & Summers 1977). We should note again that an apparently unproblematic term like reliability in physical measurement is complex and relies on measurement theory to interpret it in social science. A full discussion of the issue is beyond the scope of this book. Suffice it to say that measurement error, whether from chance (random error) or bias (systematic error), needs to be taken into account when interpreting the results of psychological tests, especially when test scores are used to make administrative or clinical decisions about individuals.

When we measure physical objects we know what we are measuring (e.g., length or width), but in psychological measurement we cannot take it for granted that we are measuring what we intend to measure. Technically speaking, we cannot be certain that our test has *construct validity*. We may, for instance, think that we are measuring spatial ability because the task requires the subject to match a particular visual pattern with another. In fact, however, we may instead be measuring verbal ability because the subject is verbalizing to himself both the elements of the pattern and how they compare to the elements of other patterns. For this reason, it is desirable to use more than one type of test to measure the same construct and to hope that the various measures converge on to the construct (convergent validity) and measure that construct exclusively (discriminant validity). The identification of underlying psychological constructs or factors has been the goal of the statistical technique known as factor analysis, to which we will now turn our attention.

FACTOR ANALYSIS

The search for one or more common factors underlying the correlations among tests or among items within a test is the goal of exploratory factor analysis. When these factors are identified, they are said to "explain" the correlations that are produced. This is because they can be considered mainly responsible for the individual differences in performance on the test, which constitute the variance obtained on the test, and entirely responsible for the covariances or correlations among tests.

The obtained or total variance of a test can be partitioned into two components: (1) the *valid variance,* which is the part it shares with other similar tests; and (2) the *unique variance,* which is the part it does not share. The unique variance can be broken down into *specific variance,* which is reliable but invalid variance, and (random) *error variance.* Tests whose total variance is made up largely of valid variance, that is, they load highly on the underlying factor(s), are deemed to possess *factorial* validity (Guilford & Hoepfner 1971), which is a favorable indication of construct validity. But before we can safely conclude that the test definitely has construct validity, we have to justify the theory in which the construct is embedded by demonstrating that hypotheses derived from the theory regarding the construct measured by the test are correct. An example will make this clearer. Suppose our test is designed to measure extroversion. According to theory, extroverts learn more slowly than introverts under conditions of massed practice. If, after sorting subjects into extroverts and introverts with the aid of the test, the hypothesis is supported, we can then be more confident that the test actually does measure extroversion. Of course, by the same token, we should also specify zero relationships with variables to which the test bears no theoretical connection. Extroverts and introverts should not differ with respect to age and social class, for example. Cronbach and Meehl (1955) refer to such a set of relationships as a *nomological network* or metatheory about measurement properties. Such a way of looking at measurement makes the point that validity is never an all-or-nothing property, as was traditionally supposed, but a relatively elusive concept, refined indefinitely as more and more evidence becomes available about the way the test works (Bynner 1988). In sum, although factorial validity is evidence of construct validity, this evidence alone is inadequate.

The factor-analytical *technique* comprises a number of different statistical approaches to grouping variables and tests and deciding which variables and tests belong to which group. These different approaches have different methods for estimating the common-factor variance or *communality* (Gorsuch 1983). The traditional approach involves accepting the correlations in a matrix at their face value (ordinary or unweighted least-squares method), whereas approaches developed subsequently attach more weight to larger correlations (generalized least-squares method, maximum-likelihood method) on the grounds that they are more reliable than smaller correlations. The latter approaches enable us to argue, given certain assumptions, that our factors would be found in the *population* from which our sample was drawn. They also allow us to test the theory about the existence of factors underlying the tests using inferential statistics such as χ^2. This is done by comparing the original sample matrix of correlations (*S*) with the matrix of population correlations implied by the factors (Σ) for goodness-of-fit. This whole procedure is utilized in confirmatory factor analysis, which is a branch of structural-equation modeling and will be discussed in more detail later in this chapter. In confirmatory factor analysis, we would specify *in advance* the number of factors in the model and possibly the variables on which they should load.

The *mathematical model* behind factor analysis is based on the notion of variance components which we have already mentioned. A score on a test is presumed to be due partly to the common factor being measured by the test and partly to a combination of a factor specific to the test and measurement error. This additive model can be expressed algebraically for a single test (X_1) in the form of a linear equation:

$$z_1 = a_1 F_1 + U_1 \tag{1}$$

where z_1 is a standard score on the test, F_1 is the hypothetical factor score, a_1 is the factor loading (that is, the standardized regression coefficient associated with the factor), and U_1 is the combined specific and error score or unique score. The square of the factor loading represents the common-factor variance or communality, meaning that a_1^2 is the proportion of total variance attributable to the factor. For three other tests (X_2, X_3, and X_4) measuring the same factor (F_1), the equations are analogous:

$$
\begin{aligned}
z_2 &= a_2F_1 + U_2 \\
z_3 &= a_3F_1 + U_3 \\
z_4 &= a_4F_1 + U_4
\end{aligned}
\tag{2}
$$

For three other tests (X_5, X_6, and X_7) measuring a *different* construct (F_2), the equations would be similar:

$$
\begin{aligned}
z_5 &= a_5F_2 + U_5 \\
z_6 &= a_6F_2 + U_6 \\
z_7 &= a_7F_2 + U_7
\end{aligned}
\tag{3}
$$

All seven equations can be summarized via matrix algebra by one equation:

$$
\mathbf{z = aF + U}
\tag{4}
$$

This matrix equation, therefore, represents four tests exclusively measuring one factor and three tests exclusively measuring another factor. These tests then show both convergent and discriminant validity. It is often the case, however, that a test will measure more than one underlying factor, thereby lacking discriminant validity. Two examples of equations for such a model are:

$$
\begin{aligned}
z_1 &= a_1F_1 + b_1F_2 + \ldots n_1F_n + U_1 \\
z_2 &= a_2F_1 + b_2F_2 + \ldots n_2F_n + U_2
\end{aligned}
\tag{5}
$$

where a_1, a_2, b_1, b_2, and so forth, are the factor loadings or regression coefficients for factors F_1 and F_2, respectively. The communality (h^2) of a test is the sum of squares of its factor loadings:

$$
\begin{aligned}
h_1^2 &= a_1^2 + b_1^2 + \ldots n_1^2 \\
h_2^2 &= a_2^2 + b_2^2 + \ldots n_2^2
\end{aligned}
\tag{6}
$$

The product-moment correlation between the two tests X_1 and X_2 equals the sum of the cross-products of their factor loadings:

$$
r_{12} = a_1a_2 + b_1b_2 + \ldots n_1n_2
\tag{7}
$$

Despite their differences, both models share the assumption that correlations between variables are produced by one or more common underlying factors. But why should they? Correlations between personal characteristics need not be the product of factors; they could be expressing *directional* relationships between them instead. In other words, verbal ability may be a prerequisite for numerical ability; to seek a common-factor explanation of their correlation may completely mask the way in which such abilities develop. It is because of such limitations of traditional factor analysis that interest has continued to grow in a whole area of statistics known as structural-equation modeling (SEM) of covariance (and correlation) matrices (Jöreskog & Sörbom 1979). SEM enables the researcher to estimate and test any identified linear model against observed data, at the same time taking measurement error into account. The exploratory techniques employed in the factor analysis of mental tests direct attention to only one such model, namely factors representing underlying dimensions, and ignore alternative possibilities. As we shall see in the next section, these alternatives include *path* models suggesting causal ordering among the tests.

ALTERNATIVE MODELS

Figure 1.1 shows four alternative ways of placing a causal interpretation on the correlation of two ability tests, T_1 and T_2.

In the absence of evidence to the contrary, all four models are equally valid explanations of the correlations, yet only one of them, model d, is upheld in the conventional factor-analytic view of ability. The unidirectional and reciprocal causal effects represented by path models b, c, and e cannot be investigated by factor analysis. If a set of tests, 1 through *n,* sharing a single common factor in varying degrees are ordered in terms of factor loadings (highest at the top, lowest at the bottom), then the correlations will decrease in size on the left-hand side of the principal diagonal and increase in size on the right-hand side of it. If, on the other hand, these tests form what is called a *simplex structure,* where the tests can be ordered into a linear sequence with one test leading causally to the next, then the correlations decrease in size from the principal diagonal to the corners of the matrix (see Figure 1.2).

The important point to note is that the possibility of a simplex structure, and consequently a linear ordering of the tests, can never be revealed by factor analysis. This method will impose a common-factor structure on the data whatever its nature. So ingrained has the factor-analytic model become in our thinking that whenever we encounter a set of highly correlated measures such as cognitive tests, we assume a common factor or factors must be responsible for them. It is only a step away

Figure 1.1
Alternative Structural Models

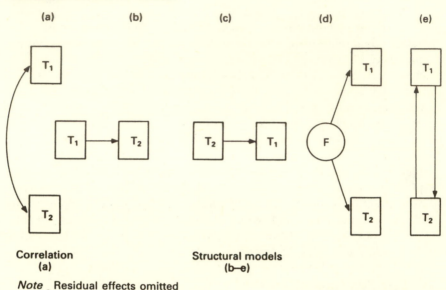

Note _ Residual effects omitted

Source: From "Intelligence, fact or artefact: Alternative structures for cognitive abilities" by J. M. Bynner and D. M. Romney, 1986, *British Journal of Educational Psychology,* *56,* p. 14. Copyright 1986 by the British Psychological Society. Reprinted by permission.

to aggregate the scores to produce a measure of "general ability," which is the most prevalent form of categorization in education.

PATH ANALYSIS

So far we have been talking about the explanation of correlation in terms of underlying factors. The alternative interpretation of them is in terms of dependency, seeing two variables as correlated with one another because they are functionally or, in theoretical terms, *causally* related to each other. The statistical model for a relationship of this kind is *regression*. Adopting the same assumptions as in factor analysis of linear relationships between variables, the relationship between a dependent variable Y and an independent or explanatory variable X is given by the formula:

$$Y = bX + c \tag{8}$$

where b is a regression coefficient and c is a constant. In terms of stan-

Figure 1.2
Factor and Simplex Correlation Structure

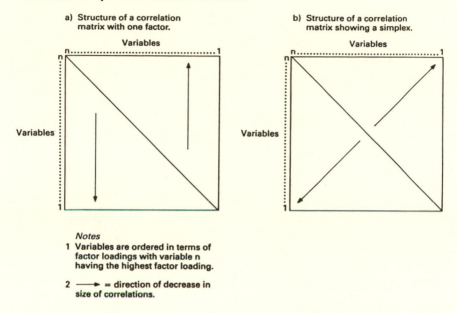

a) Structure of a correlation
matrix with one factor.

b) Structure of a correlation
matrix showing a simplex.

Notes
1 Variables are ordered in terms of
factor loadings with variable n
having the highest factor loading.

2 ⟶ = direction of decrease in
size of correlations.

Source: From "Intelligence, fact or artefact: Alternative structures for cognitive abilities" by
J. M. Bynner and D. M. Romney, 1986, *British Journal of Educational Psychology,*
56, p. 15. Copyright 1986 by the British Psychological Society. Reprinted by permission.

dardized measurements for each variable (z scores), the equation becomes:

$$z_y = \beta z_x \tag{9}$$

where β is the standardized regression coefficient. With only one dependent and independent variable, β also equals the product-moment correlation coefficient (r) between X and Y. Thus, if our two variables are verbal ability (Y) and social class (X), then the regression coefficient of Y on X can be interpreted as the strength of the causal relationship between verbal ability and social class, with social class determining verbal ability. We stress "*can* be interpreted" because, as in factor analysis, mere existence of correlation does not prove causality. On the other hand, if there is a causal relationship as postulated by theory, the existence of correlation is a necessary, but not sufficient, condition.

This bare principle underpins the theory-testing strategy known as *path analysis*. Given that a number of variables (Y) are related causally as in

Figure 1.3
Path-Analysis Model

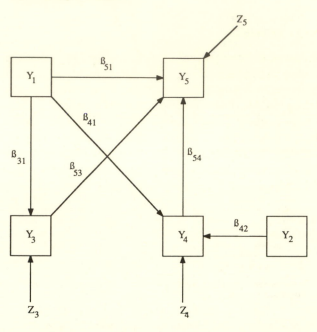

Figure 1.3., then regression coefficients, known as *path coefficients* when causality is implied, are expressed algebraically as follows:

$$Y_3 = \beta_{31} Y_1 + Z_3 \tag{10}$$
$$Y_4 = \beta_{41} Y_1 + \beta_{42} Y_2 + Z_4$$
$$Y_5 = \beta_{54} Y_4 + \beta_{53} Y_3 + \beta_{51} Y_1 + Z_5$$

where the Zs are residuals (i.e., parts of the scores that cannot be predicted or explained by the preceding variables). All other regression coefficients calculated between the Ys should be zero or, at the very least, statistically insignificant. If these predictions fail to be borne out by the data, the causal theory from which the path model was derived must be wrong. Again, as in factor analysis, we can summarize sets of path equations by a single matrix equation.

$$\mathbf{Y} = \mathbf{BY} + \mathbf{Z} \tag{11}$$

Note that in Figure 1.3 all the arrows go in one direction. This means there is no mutual dependency or reciprocal causation. Such a set of relationships are designated as a set of *recursive* relationships. Conversely, when there *is* reciprocal causation, the relationships are said to be *nonrecursive*.

COMBINED MODEL

Recognition of the common basis of factor analysis and path analysis in what is known as the general linear model stimulated the attempt to bring them together into a single theory-testing framework—structural-equation modeling (SEM). The attraction of SEM is that it is able to bring the factor or measurement model and the path or structural model, two separate models, together into a single model (see Figure 1.4). It can also be used to analyze data from several groups simultaneously (cf. ANOVA).

A set of nine variables, xs and ys, are used to operationalize three theoretical variables, F_1, f_1, and f_2, which are related in terms of the

Figure 1.4
Combined Model

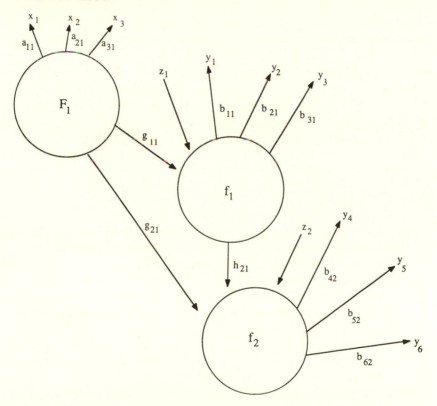

Note: Measurement error terms omitted.

causal pattern shown in Figure 1.4. The xs and ys are scored in deviation units, with the means subtracted from the raw scores. It is the convention for the xs to represent the observed indicators of the exogenous factors (F), and for the ys to represent the observed indicators of the endogenous variables (f). The following is the full set of matrix equations for the model:

$$\mathbf{x} = \mathbf{aF} + \mathbf{d} \tag{12}$$

$$\mathbf{y} = \mathbf{bf} + \mathbf{e} \tag{13}$$

$$\mathbf{f} = \mathbf{hf} + \mathbf{gF} + \mathbf{z} \tag{14}$$

where a is the vector of the factor loadings for F on x, and d is the vector of measurement error component (unique variance) of x. Note that for each endogenous f there is a residual variance z, for each indicator y there is a residual error term e, and for each indicator x there is a residual error term d. In more familiar terminology, including ds and es in the model corrects the structural parameters, a and h, for attenuation. The variances of the zs in the model indicate part of the variance of each latent or endogenous latent variable that cannot be explained by the variables preceding it in the causal chain.

A basic assumption of the model is that for each latent variable the residual terms and the error terms do not correlate with the factor or with each other; that is, the zs do not correlate with the es. Error terms can correlate with each other, however; likewise, residuals can correlate with each other. Including such correlations in the model provides another means of improving the estimates of the structural (causal) parameters with which the theory is primarily concerned. An important generalization is that the model applies regardless of how many observed variables are considered necessary to measure F. In the simplest case of only one observed variable, F is no more than x corrected for measurement error, and the (internal consistency) reliability of x becomes the variance of the factor (i.e., the factor loading squared, a^2). In the ideal situation where the theoretical variable F is perfectly measured, d is zero, a is 1, and F and x are identical (see equation 12).

Finally, the model is not restricted to recursive relations; nonrecursive or reciprocal dependencies among the endogenous variables can be encompassed within it. For example, f_2 can be postulated as dependent on f_1 which is simultaneously dependent on f_2; that is, $f_1 \rightleftarrows f_2$. The capability of "dynamic modeling," which is not simple to achieve with conventional path analysis, is another valuable feature of SEM.

A number of SEM programs have been developed, such as LISREL (Jöreskog & Sörbom 1989), EQS (Bentler 1985), and COSAN (McDonald 1980). These differ in the range of facilities they provide the investigator with for specifying the model, diagnosing faults in it, and testing its good-ness-of-fit to the data. The first one to be made available was LISREL, which is now in its seventh version and is a supplementary procedure to SPSS-X. It has been widely used across a range of disciplines in social science, especially in North America, prompting Cliff to refer to LISREL as "perhaps the most important and influential statistical revolution to have occurred in the Social Sciences . . . since the adoption of analysis of variance in the 1940's." For a nontechnical introduction, see Bynner and Romney (1985) or Saris and Stronkhorst (1984). EQS is also well known and is associated with the package of statistical programs known as BMD-P. The main advantage of the latter over LISREL is that it does not require a knowledge of matrix algebra (as LISREL does) and does not use Greek symbols to represent (population) parameters.

The main features of the LISREL system in testing a model are the following:

1. For parameters of the model to be capable of estimation, they must be uniquely determined by the observed data; that is to say, the set of simultaneous equations expressing the model must have only one solu-tion. Under this condition the model is said to be "identified." To achieve identification certain parameters in the model (e.g., factor loadings, path coefficients, or variances) can be constrained at zero or to some other fixed value, or can be made to be equal to one another. For example, in principle all the indicators in Figure 1.4 could have loadings on all the factors; the constraints imposed on the measurement model force large numbers of these factor loadings to be zero, as theory dictates. When the model is not identified, the program finds the particular parameter that is causing the problem. But to ensure identification for complex models, it is also often necessary to work through the algebra (Duncan 1975 gives a detailed account).

2. After preliminary estimation of optimum start values, the program estimates the parameters of the models iteratively by maximum like-lihood methods under conditions of best fit. This means that the dif-ference between the correlations (or covariances) implied by the param-eters and the observed correlations (or covariances)—the residual correlation matrix—will be minimized.

3. Under the condition of multivariate normality for the distribution of the observed variables, a statistical (likelihood ratio) test, χ^2, is available to test how closely the residual correlation matrix is to zero. In a highly constrained model in which many parameters are set to zero, χ^2 relative to degrees of freedom is liable to be large. Releasing the constraints on certain parameters will reduce χ^2 relative to degrees of freedom; and as parameters continue to be released, a χ^2 approaching zero can be achieved. However, there is a danger in proceeding too far in this direc-tion. "Overfitting" not only capitalizes on chance but distorts the pur-

poses of scientific theorizing, which has as its aim the most parsimonious explanation of observed phenomena in terms of the minimum number of explanatory (theoretical) constructs. In other words, the number of parameters to estimate needs to be minimized.

4. It is the practice in LISREL work, typically, to decide on a reasonable χ^2 value relative to degrees of freedom as an index of fit, alongside other indices of fit such as a goodness-of-fit index (with a range of 0 to 1) and the observed residual (normalized) correlations either averaged or used by choosing a maximum value. Ways of introducing a more rigorous approach to testing in LISREL have frequently been discussed (e.g., Bentler & Bonnett 1980; Hoelter 1983). The problem in using them is that only poor approximations to multivariate normality are likely to be achieved with most observed data. Goodness-of-fit tests also suffer from the problem that the size of χ^2 depends critically on sample size, which means that, in large sample work, a good fit of a constrained model on strictly statistical criteria is virtually impossible to achieve without overfitting the model.

5. Diagnostic information is obtained whereby the equivalent of χ^2 values are attached to particular parameters constrained to be zero. The modification index generated, for example, for each parameter constrained to be zero indicates how much the overall χ^2 will be reduced by releasing the constraint on the parameter. The matrix of residual correlations is also supplied, pointing to those correlations in the original data that the model has been least successful in explaining.

6. Some data may not conform to the basic assumption of interval measurement (for product-moment correlation) and multivariate normality (for the distributions of all the measured variables). In the latest versions of LISREL, polychoric and polyserial correlations can be computed as well as product-moment correlations. These are generalizations of the familiar tetrachoric and biserial correlations and enable categorical and ordinal variables as well as intervals to be included in the model. Moreover, other estimation methods—generalized least squares and unweighted least squares—are also included as alternatives to maximum likelihood estimation. These may be preferred, particularly when the assumption of multivariate normality is violated.

CONCLUSIONS

Throughout this chapter our discussion has been concerned mainly with the theoretical question of what is the best way to account for correlations among personal characteristics. But practical questions are also bound up with the interpretation of correlations. To conceptualize abilities as residing ultimately in a single characteristic, intelligence, leads almost inevitably to a genetic conception of human potential. In fact,

Spearman's main aim in developing factor analysis was to test Galton's genetic theory of intelligence (Richardson & Bynner 1984). Genetic theories push educators towards classification and selection of children for different educational tracks because such theories assume that the characteristics of children are relatively fixed. In contrast, linear sequences exemplified by the simplex model emphasize dynamic change. Fixed factorial conceptions lead to one form of practice; fluid simplex patterns lead to another. Similarly, in psychiatry today, the scene is dominated by the medical tradition of diagnosing fixed syndromes or clusters of symptoms that are regarded as being qualitatively different from normal behavior and to which we may be predisposed genetically, rather than viewing abnormal behavior as an extreme form of behavior lying on a continuum of behaviors that are influenced by the environment. If we are able to show that a psychiatric disorder such as paranoia develops sequentially along the lines of a simplex, the implications for treatment will be quite different than those stemming from the medical paradigm (see Romney 1987).

Through the influence of psychologists, much of education and clinical practice has been dominated by fixed factorial conceptions and a narrow view of practice. The application of SEM to personal characteristics may be seen as helping to liberate practitioners from this too narrow view of human potential and performance. In place of fixed factors, we have sequences of abilities or traits, each of which may give rise to any of the others. Provided that teaching is directed in the right way to the right ability (i.e., at the beginning of the sequence), all of the abilities are likely to grow. Such reasoning applies equally in psychotherapy to improve personal adjustment and functioning, and in communications to bring about attitude change. The choice of models in the different domains is not just of interest to academics but crucial to policy and practice.

The technicalities of SEM, which put some researchers off from using it, are less important than the scientific principles that underlie it. The conventional methods of multivariate statistics tie theory to a limited set of interpretations of observed data. But the very language in which these interpretations are expressed often disguises this fact. People talk about "discovering" factors or "explaining" variance, content with the theoretical commitment that such statements imply, yet typically unaware of how *model-bound* the evidence is on which they are based. Three separate research traditions have become associated with particular statistical models in this way. The science of mental measurement, psychometrics, has relied almost exclusively on factor analysis as the means of validating its theoretical constructs. In contrast, econometrics relies on multiple regression theory to model relationships between variables; the emphasis is on predicting and explaining effects that variables have on other variables that are assumed to be perfectly measured. Finally, experimental psychologists have employed analysis of variance to analyze the results of experiments to ascertain overall effects of varying conditions on the mean values of a dependent variable by partitioning the variance among various sources.

In their own ways, these methods can do a lot to help the researcher answer the specific questions a theory generates. *What they do not do is enable the theory to be tested as a whole.* By bringing together all the statistical methods derived from the general linear model into a single testing framework, SEM enables the theory to be evaluated and its deficiencies to be recognized. The next step is reappraisal and reconceptualization at every level: the operationalization of the concepts involved, their functional relations with each other, and the effects on them that need to be controlled. SEM does not prove theory, any more than it demonstrates causality; nor in itself does it provide an alternative theory when the existing one fails. Its main aid is as a stimulus to scientific reasoning, a key to unlock the intellectual straitjacket in which conventional approaches have encased too much of social science in the past. This is not to say that SEM will necessarily provide better explanations of human performance than those advanced in the past, but it should open up new possibilities.

Chapter 2

Abilities: Hierarchies Versus Processes

ABILITIES AND INTELLIGENCE

Of all the personal characteristics, abilities have probably received the most attention. Interest in the origins of the distribution of power and status in society, not to mention occupational roles and hierarchies, leads to ideas of personal aptitude overriding family background and subsequent experience. We observe that one child spontaneously comes up with a novel solution to a reasoning problem while another makes no progress with it; we see some secondary-school students racing ahead of others en route to higher education; we marvel at the endeavors of brilliant musicians, scientists, and military strategists. The specific personal attributes associated with these achievements are typically referred to as abilities. These are the main focus of this chapter.

Nunnally (1978) defines abilities as "individual differences in how well people perform different tasks when they try" (501). This definition carries certain assumptions with it that Nunnally makes explicit. The first is that abilities concern individual differences. Certain species-specific abilities—to speak, to walk upright, to swim—are abilities that, given certain environmental conditions and experience, all human beings can acquire; it is in the facility with which people exercise these abilities that our interest lies. Secondly, abilities relate to tasks, or better, classes of tasks. Some people may be good at running and others at writing. Broadly we can classify abilities into two types: first, intellectual or cognitive abilities that involve thinking and reasoning (usually but not exclusively from a basis of prior knowledge) and that may be expected to have an important role in educational achievements; and second, special abilities that involve the use of such skills as mechanical aptitude, artistic and creative skills, and physical prowess. It is the former types of ability to which research and theory have been most extensively applied and that again will concern us most here. Finally, the phrase "if they try" in Nunnally's definition assumes that people are driven by another personal characteristic, motivation. We have to assume that all individuals want to succeed in mastering a task if we are to be able to differentiate their ability to do so.

The central problems that research has been directed at resolving in relation to abilities are the following:

1. Are abilities inherited or acquired through learning?
2. Are there many or just a few primary abilities, or even only one intelligence, from which all the others arise?
3. Does the possession of one ability influence the possession of another?

The answers to these questions are interconnected in the sense that a particular view about the answer to question one, namely that abilities are inherited, leads to theories about underlying genotypes and consequently about ability hierarchies. The alternative view that abilities are acquired through experience or that there is no meaningful way of separating out any inherited component leads more readily to the belief that the relations among abilities are dynamic, with each one influencing others through the processes of maturing and learning.

Nevertheless, we are not going to concern ourselves with the heritability question, which has been exhaustively reviewed and argued about elsewhere (e.g., Goldberger 1979; Jensen 1980; Keating 1984; Kempthorne 1978; Richardson & Bynner 1984). We will focus on the competing theoretical positions represented in questions two and three and on how structural equation modeling (SEM) can help us to adjudicate between them.

FACTOR MODELS OF ABILITY

The origins of the factor model of cognitive abilities stretches back to the mid-nineteenth century, when Francis Galton attempted to operationalize his theory of intelligence. Drawing on the ideas of Herbert Spencer, Galton (1884) conceived of the superior intellects of successful people as having a physical substrate originating in heredity. It follows that parents are able to pass their abilities on to their children. As Spencer put it (1855): "Those having well developed nervous systems will display a relatively marked premeditation—an habitual representation of more various possibilities of cause and conduct and consequence—a greater tendency to suspense of judgments and an easier modification of judgments that have been formed" (581).

The belief that intelligence resided in more effective "nervous systems" pointed to such measures as reaction time and visual acuity as the means of operationalizing it. The theory predicted that these physical attributes would be related to each other and to educational performance; and a junior colleague of Galton, Charles Spearman, applied the statistical method of correlation to measure the strength of the relationships. This early line of research led nowhere, however, as the predicted correlations failed to materialize. But the basic physical metaphors, such as mental capacity, mental efficiency, and mental energy, carried over from it. The program turned inevitably to those measures that did predict performance, various mental problems of the kind that educational tests themselves often comprised. In France, Binet adopted this approach in his early work at the end of the last century. Later, with Simon, he developed the famous Binet–Simon test designed to identify children with mental retardation, which similarly relied on mental problems for the children to solve. Five of the problems taken from the twenty that Binet and Simon originally devised in 1905 for their test are shown below (Binet & Simon 1905). The problems retain connections with physical attributes (e.g., items 1 and 2); but the main emphasis is now on mental processes, recognizing, memorizing, and defining:

1. Touch head, nose, ear, cap, key, straw.
2. Judge which of two lines is longer.
3. Repeat three digits read by an examiner.
4. Define house, horse, fork.
5. Repeat sentence of fifteen words after a single hearing.

Interestingly, Binet's test was directed more at determining what kind of educational help children with low scores needed to raise their intelligence, that is, as an aid to diagnosis of their learning problems rather than as a means of identifying any fixed limits on their potential for intellectual growth (Keating 1984). Terman in the United States, who adapted Binet's test for American use—the Stanford-Binet test—and Spearman in Britain, working on more tightly specified cognitive tasks in Britain, pursued this latter, more theoretically oriented, agenda. In the tradition of Galton, they viewed such intelligence tests as the means of measuring the fixed potential of individuals for learning. Mental testing was a means not of determining what educational assistance an individual needed but of deciding what was the appropriate curriculum for people of different (fixed) levels of cognitive ability. The developing forms of industrial organization and automated production processes harmonized particularly well with this latter view: People of "inferior mentality" could be put to work under the direction of others with superior intellects. "One man with ability to think and plan guides the labor often of twenty laborers who do what they are told to do and have little need for resourcefulness and initiative" (Terman 1919, 276).

The basic data for research on cognitive abilities in this research tradition are the correlations among the scores for a sample of individuals on a number of ability tests. As we saw in the previous chapter, there are many ways to explain correlations, each of which implies a different explanatory model for the data. As has been already pointed out, the dominant tradition of cognitive ability research pursued one of these models at the expense of others—the hierarchical or factor model of ability. It is a well-established fact, and one that such proponents as Jensen (1980) make much of, that all of the vast range of tests to measure cognitive abilities invariably produce relatively high intercorrelations. In one sense this is not surprising because either directly or indirectly they all comprise test items that tap various forms of educational performance. But the point we wish to stress here is that whether they show low, moderate, or consistently high intercorrelations is completely irrelevant to the issue of the appropriate model to explain them.

Spearman interpreted the intercorrelations of cognitive ability tests as providing evidence for the existence of Galton's general factor of intelligence. In what was the first formulation of factor analysis, Spearman (1904) showed, in terms of a simple linear model, how the correlations could be explained if each test were considered to share a common general factor, g, with other tests and to have a specific factor unique, s, to itself. The model for five such tests, y_1, y_2, y_3, y_4, and y_5, is set out below where g is the general factor and s_1, s_2, s_3, s_4, and s_5 are specific factors and e_1, e_2, e_3, e_4, and e_5 are measurement errors.

$$y_1 = a_1g + s_1 + e_1 \tag{1}$$

$$y_2 = a_2g + s_2 + e_2 \tag{2}$$

$$y_3 = a_3g + s_3 + e_3 \tag{3}$$

$$y_4 = a_4g + s_4 + e_4 \tag{4}$$

$$y_5 = a_5g + s_5 + e_5 \tag{5}$$

In practice the s and e are not usually treated separately in this model but, as we saw in chapter 1, are combined together as the "uniqueness" (u).

$$\mathbf{y} = \mathbf{a}g + \mathbf{u} \tag{6}$$

For the model to be supported by the data, the consequence of partialing out the effect of g from the correlations among the ys must be to reduce them to zero. For this condition to hold, it can be shown by simple algebra (see chapter 1) that the correlations (r) need to conform to a particular pattern of proportionality:

$$r_{13}/r_{23} = r_{14}/r_{24} = r_{15}/r_{25} \tag{7}$$

Using this criterion, known as Spearman's "Tetrad Difference" test, inspection of a correlation matrix can enable the researcher to ascertain fairly easily whether a general factor underlies the tests. In his later work, Spearman (1927) acknowledged that sets of correlations among ability measures conforming with this principle were rare, and he recognized the need for "group factors" to account for the correlations. These group factors could be considered to underlie *some* ability measures and not others. As we shall see, all this meant was that another layer in the hierarchy had to be added to account adequately for the correlations. General intelligence, *g*, could still be considered to be ultimately the basis of all of them.

Perhaps because his work was carried out in the United States, where, apart from Terman, generally less hierarchical views of social organization prevailed, the approach of the other early founder of factor analysis, Thurstone, was less tied to the pursuit of Galton's theoretical ideas. Thurstone's multiple-group factor model dispensed with the idea of a single general factor and specific factors in favor of a set of "primary ability" group factors underlying all cognitive tests. The scores on each test can be attributed, in terms of the linear model shown below, to one or more such group factors and measurement error alone.

y_1, y_2, y_3, y_4, and y_5 are the tests, F_1 and F_2 are two group factors and e_1, e_2, e_3, e_4, and e_5 are measurement errors:

$$y_1 = a_1F_1 + e_1 \tag{8}$$

$$y_2 = a_2F_1 + e_2 \tag{9}$$

$$y_3 = b_3F_2 + e_3 \tag{10}$$

$$y_4 = b_4F_2 + e_4 \tag{11}$$

$$y_5 = b_5F_2 + e_5 \tag{12}$$

Thurstone's research, carried out with his wife, was on a much larger scale than that of his predecessors. In one of his major studies, he employed sixty tests with 1,100 school children and concluded that six factors in the tests could be clearly identified: (1) verbal comprehension (V); (2) fluency (W); (3) number (N); (4) space (S); (5) rote memory (M); and (6) inductive reasoning (R). Two more factors were less clearly defined: a perceptual factor (P) and deductive reasoning (D). Spearman's factors were, by definition, uncorrelated with each other. To optimize the fit of the factors to the test data, Thurstone developed the idea of "simple structure" in factor analysis, allowing the factors to be oblique, that is, correlated.

Factors can be represented geometrically as the axes defining a multidimensional space in which all of the original variables (the mental tests) are represented by vectors with a common origin. The angle of separation between two vectors represents the correlation between the two variables, whereas the angle of separation between a vector and a factor represents a factor loading (angle = 0°, $r = 1$; angle = 90°, $r = 0$; angle = 180°, $r = -1$; angle = 270°, $r = 0$). The principle of simple structure requires the axes to be rotated to those positions in the multidimensional space that align the axes with "bundles" of closely related vectors, thus maximizing the loadings for the variables to which each factor relates and minimizing the loadings for all the other variables. This can be achieved either under the condition that the factors remain uncorrelated with each other (orthogonal rotation) or, meeting Thurstone's full requirements for simple structure, under the condition that they are allowed to become correlated (oblique rotation).

The existence of correlations among the primary ability factors raised the question for Thurstone of whether deeper factors could not be considered to underlie them. In later studies, second-order factors were produced, bringing Thurstone's model closer to Spearman's. Subsequently, Vernon and Cattell independently formulated the hierarchical factor model incorporating both Spearman's and Thurstone's factor models, with group factors at the bottom and one or more general factors at the top (Figure 2.1).

Vernon (1950) retained Spearman's general factor g at the top of the hierarchy but concluded that two general factors were needed below it: *v:ed*, concerned with all those skills acquired through and utilized in education, including verbal and mathematics skills; and *k:m*, concerned with perceptual and spatial factors that seemed largely impervious to educational effects. In parallel, Cattell (1963) made the distinction at the top of his hierarchy between what he called "fluid" and "crystallized" intelligence. Tests of fluid intelligence demand the ability to see often complex relationships between relatively simple elements: number series and letter series, figure classification, figure analogies, and so on. Tests of crystallized intelligence have informational content and draw on the subject's already acquired knowledge and skills, general information, vocabulary, numerical information, and mechanical information.

Such hierarchies have gained general acceptance among psychometricians. The most sophisticated version is probably that of Guilford (Guilford & Hoepfner 1971). Pursuing the idea of primary abilities much further than Thurstone had, Guilford postulated a three-fold classification of factors in terms of five "operations," six types of "product," and four types of "content," from which he deduced that 120 factors were needed to account for the whole cognitive ability domain (see Figure 2.2). These factors embrace hierarchies of abilities at different levels within content areas, as seen in the model of "productive thinking" shown in Figure 2.3.

There are two points to be made about the research that we have considered so far. First, the methodology involved is what has now come

Figure 2.1
Factor Hierarchies

Diagram showing the hierarchical relationship among factors that may emerge from a factor analysis of a number of diverse tests each composed of highly similar (homogenous) items.

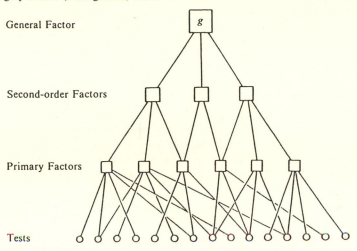

General Factor

Second-order Factors

Primary Factors

Tests

Vernon's hierarchical model of the organization of ability factors. g = general factor, $v{:}ed$ = verbal-educational aptitude, $k{:}m$ = spatial-mechanical aptitude.

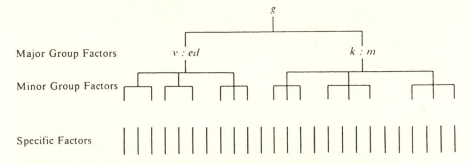

Major Group Factors $v : ed$ $k : m$

Minor Group Factors

Specific Factors

Figure 2.2
Guilford's Structure-of-Intellect Model

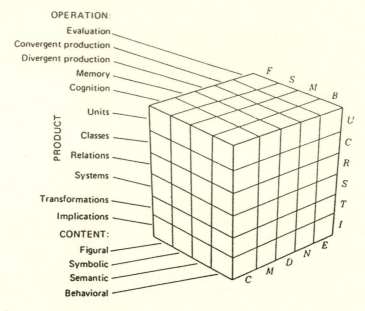

Source: From *Psychometric Theory* by J. C. Nunnally, 1978, New York: McGraw-Hill, Inc. Figure 13.2. Copyright 1978 by McGraw-Hill, Inc. Reprinted by permission.

to be called "exploratory factor analysis" (EFA). Although a particular model is implicit in the technique (i.e., one or more underlying factors explaining correlations), indeterminacy in testing it and in deriving the factor loadings for the variables involved is apparent in a variety of ways. As we saw in chapter 1, EFA provides a framework for developing models of a certain kind, but cannot determine unambiguously which one of these models is correct.

1. There is no single answer to the question of how many factors are needed to account for the correlations at any given level in the factor hierarchy; nor to the question of how many levels there should be.

2. It remains unclear to which positions the factors should ideally be "rotated" in the multidimensional space which they form: Should they be orthogonal, maintaining independence from each other? Or should they be oblique or interdependent, meeting the requirements of simple structure? If the latter, what is the optimal way achieving simple structure?

3. The lumping of specific factors and measurement errors together in the factor model to form the "uniqueness" (u) means that an estimate of how much variance in each variable is unique and how much is due to

Figure 2.3
Guilford's Hierarchical Model of Productive Thinking

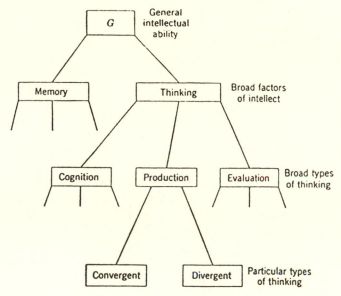

Source: From *Psychometric Theory* by J. C. Nunnally, 1978, New York: McGraw-Hill, Inc. Figure 13.5. Copyright 1978 by McGraw-Hill, Inc. Reprinted by permission.

common factors (communality) has to be made *before* the analysis begins. The solution varies from assuming that all the variance is communality to using some kind of reliability estimate for every variable or its squared multiple correlation with every other variable.

The above are statistical problems for which numerous technical solutions are available. The more difficult substantive issue relates to the cognitive theory that is implied. The theory behind factors attaches theoretical significance to different ways of classifying the content of cognitive ability tests. This theory ignores cognitive processes, both the developmental processes by which one ability becomes transformed into another and the process by which each different ability grows. It has periodically been stressed (e.g., Anastasi 1983; Cronbach 1970; Sternberg 1985; Thurstone 1938), but more frequently disregarded, that factor analysis has less to do with the discovery of basic mental properties than with classifying different mental test performances. Strong theory is, therefore, required to choose between different classifications, or to dispense with them altogether in favor of a different approach to making sense of the data. The former position is best exemplified by the "componential" theory advanced by Sternberg (1977, 1980, 1985). While still relying on the notion of individual differences along what are now called "intelligence components," it places a much greater emphasis on the cognitive processes involved in cognitive functioning, distinguishing three types of processes: (1) "metacomponents" are concerned with the ability to select the right strategy to tackle a test item; (2) "knowledge acquisition components"—acquisition, retention, and transfer—are concerned with learning what needs to be done; and (3) "performance components" are concerned with how well the cognitive tasks are actually performed. Much of the work conducted in the Thurstone tradition of primary abilities is in the domain of performance components, whereas Spearman's interest in higher-level processes—"the eduction of correlates and differences"— places g in the domain of the metacomponents. But the most distinctive feature of Sternberg's system is that relations between components within and between sets are not seen to reside in genotypes as theorists from Spearman (1904) to Jensen (1980) have argued, but are perceived as dynamic and interactive, so that influence flows from the performance and knowledge components back to the metacomponents in continuous feedback loops. This dynamic aspect of Sternberg's system gives it a particular appeal which we shall return to. At this point, we need to note only that for Sternberg the idea of components is still central to the explanation of cognitive test performance and that the evidence presented in support of components is mainly experimental.

The *structural-equation modeling* approach (SEM), which we turn to next, enables both competing models in the factor-theory tradition to be put to a precise test. SEM also enables us to consider models embracing more process-oriented alternative possibilities of the Sternberg kind.

ALTERNATIVES TO THE FACTOR MODEL

What alternatives are there to the idea that cognitive abilities are generated by factors? Alternatives reside in the other models considered in chapter 1: recursive or causal models, in which one ability as measured by a test is considered to influence the others; and nonrecursive, dynamic models in which both abilities are considered to influence each other.

Use of the terminology of causal path analysis, with the emphasis on causal explanation and influence, is in the tradition of work with the general linear model as developed through factor analysis and structural-equation modeling. But an earlier alternative to the factor conception suggested dispensing with this language altogether. Louis Guttman's approach (Guttman 1954) focused on the rank orders of correlations and how these could be reflected in different structures. Thus, the "simplex" is reflected in correlations that decrease from the principal diagonal of the correlation matrix to the corners; the "circumplex" is shown by correlations that decrease initially and then increase towards the corners of the matrix. A "radex" comprises circumplexes of tests of comparable complexity and simplexes of tests varying in complexity in particular content domains.

Formulation of these simplexes, circumplexes, and radexes involves monotonic transformation of rank orders into a topological space, a form of what is called multidimensional scaling (MDS). This draws on ideas derived from the analysis of similarity/dissimilarity data matrices, whereby simple dimensional representation of stimulus objects can be achieved in which the only requirement is that the rank order relation between the objects in the space formed by the dimensions is maintained. Thus if two cars are judged more like each other than a third, then after the scaling transformation this relationship must be preserved. Applied to correlation matrices of ability-test data, Guttman's approach treats the correlations as indices of similarity and dissimilarity and the metric properties of the variables involved are ignored. This rules out interpretation in terms of the general linear model and consequently its use to partition and predict variance as in factor analysis and regression.

In factor analysis, the axes of the multidimensional factor space are the factors to which theoretical attention is directed. In the topological space in which Guttman's structures are located, no significance is attached to the axes defining the space. The whole concern is with the relations between tests within the space. The diagram (Figure 2.4), taken from an account of a modern analysis of ability-test data using Guttman's methods (Snow, Kyllonen, & Marshalek 1984), shows the parallelism of the two approaches. Spearman's *g* factor at the top of an ability hierarchy now gives way to basic cognitive processes at the center of a set of concentric circles corresponding to more complex combinations of cognitive operations at increasing levels of complexity. In ability-test terms, supposedly "pure" measures of *g* such as Raven's Progressive Matrices are at the center of the circle and tests of the kind used to assess school performance are on the perimeter.

Our own approach is to stay within the metric traditions of the general linear model on which factor analysis rests but to explore alternatives to factor analysis. Thus we seek linear dependencies with predictive power, for use in explaining variance in ability-test scores. This seems to us to lead more obviously to new directions for practice.

Proponents of factor models typically assume that it is possible to establish through tests the limits of cognitive growth and consequently the curricula appropriate to particular individuals (e.g., Jensen 1980). In a more dynamic linear model, we hope to identify where, among a set of causally related abilities, influence from outside is likely to produce the

Figure 2.4
Radex vs. Hierarchy

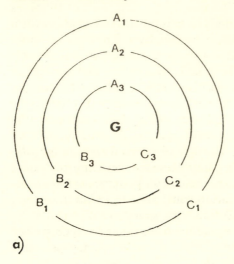

a)

	G	A	B	C
A₁	1	3	0	0
A₂	2	4	0	0
A₃	3	3	1	1
B₁	1	0	3	0
B₂	2	0	4	0
B₃	3	1	3	1
C₁	1	0	0	3
C₂	2	0	0	4
C₃	3	1	1	3
G	4	2	2	2

b)

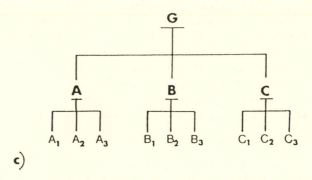

c)

Hypothetical example of radex and hierarchical model parallelism: a) a radex scaling for ten tests; b) the associated hierarchical factor matrix; c) the associated hierarchical factor diagram.

largest effects. The advantage of models relying on variance explanation is that they yield precise estimates of the predictable consequences of changes in practice which can then be evaluated empirically.

ANALYSIS OF RICHMOND TESTS OF BASIC SKILLS

To illustrate this approach we apply a variety of structural-equation models to data collected in a school in Birmingham, England, using the Richmond Tests of Basic Skills (Hieronymus & Lindquist 1967; France 1975). These tests, which are widely used in educational monitoring, are intended to provide a profile of cognitive skills measured by tests in eleven content areas. The tests were used over a number of years in the Birmingham school, with up to 400 children taking them each year. The data initially examined here were pooled over three years from 1,075 eleven-to-twelve-year-old children. The school selected eight of the tests for monitoring: vocabulary, reading comprehension, spelling, capitalization, punctuation, grammatical usage, mathematics concepts, and mathematics problem solving. The correlation matrix for the children's scores in the eight tests is shown in Table 2.1. To compare alternative and structural equation models, we first examined the factor model and then alternative path models.

Table 2.1
Correlations Between the Richmond Tests

		1	2	3	4	5	6	7	8
Vocabulary	1.	1.00							
Comprehension	2.	.77	1.00						
Spelling	3.	.62	.65	1.00					
Capitalization	4.	.56	.61	.66	1.00				
Punctuation	5.	.52	.58	.63	.64	1.00			
Usage	6.	.64	.69	.65	.62	.61	1.00		
Math concepts	7.	.61	.62	.58	.55	.54	.53	1.00	
Math problems	8.	.51	.53	.54	.48	.48	.44	.69	1.00

FACTOR-ANALYSIS MODEL

The correlation matrix in Table 2.1 has the typical features of those originally examined by Spearman, Thurstone, and the numerous other ability analysts who have followed them. Uniformly high intercorrelation among the tests suggests that all of them may be measuring much the same thing, generalized intellectual ability or intelligence. Exploratory factor analysis gives some credence to this interpretation.

One common "rule of thumb" is that a general factor explanation of correlation should not be applied unless the ratio of the variance explained by the first principal component of the matrix to the variance explained by the second is over six (Harman 1967). In this case the ratio is eight. On the other hand, close inspection of the correlations suggests a degree of clustering of the verbal as opposed to the mathematics tests, with relatively higher correlations within the two sets than between them. Separate factors for the verbal and mathematics tests conform to Thurstone's separation of them in his original eight-fold classification of abilities. So we have two alternative factor models to test: a general factor model in which all the intercorrelations among the tests can be accounted for by one general factor and specific factors for each test, and an alternative two-factor model separating out the verbal tests from the mathematical tests. Table 2.2 shows the result of fitting each of these two models (single-factor and two-factor) to the test data by means of LISREL.

Each model was evaluated in two forms: first in a highly constrained form exactly as specified by the model (a), and second in a less constrained form, with residuals between some of the specified variables free to correlate (b). Indications of which residual correlations would be most

Table 2.2
Goodness-of-Fit Statistics for Factor Models

Model	χ^2	df	GFI	RMS
1a	χ^2 too large to be calculated			
1b	101.32	17	.975	.024
2a	256.02	19	.933	.033
2b	53.41	17	.979	.049

Notes:
  Model 1a constrains all correlations between residuals to be zero.
  Model 1b releases the constraints on three of the correlations between residuals.
  Model 2a has no overlapping between the factors and no correlations between residuals.
  Model 2b has overlap on variable 6 (usage) and releases the constraints on three of the correlations between residuals e_1e_2, e_3e_4, e_4e_5.

likely to improve the fit of the model came from the LISREL diagnostic information. Figure 2.5 shows the parameter estimates, including factor loadings and residuals, for model 2b.

The goodness-of-fit indices employed to evaluate the fit of each model to the data are χ^2 relative to degrees of freedom, the goodness-of-fit index (GFI) and the root mean square residual (RMS). These last two indices of

Figure 2.5
Factor Model 2b

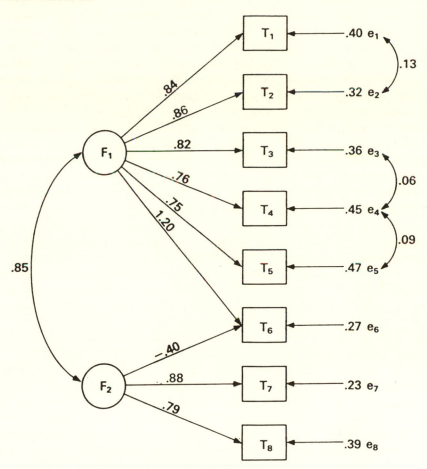

Key: F = factor, T = test, e = residual variance.

Source: From "Intelligence, fact or artefact: Alternative structures for cognitive abilities" by J. M. Bynner and D. M. Romney, 1986, *British Journal of Educational Psychology, 56,* p. 17. Copyright 1986 by the British Psychological Society. Reprinted by permission.

fit reflect the amount of covariance in the data explained by the model and are less affected by sample size than are some other measures of fit (Marsh, Balla, & McDonald 1988). Chi-square, on the other hand, is strongly sensitive to sample size and is most likely to suggest a poor fit when the sample is large.

In evaluating the fit of different models, we seek goodness-of-fit indices that are as close to unity as possible, root mean square residuals which are as close to zero as possible and χ^2 values relative to degrees of freedom which are as small as possible. Ultimately we would seek a χ^2 that is no larger than the degrees of freedom to which it relates. In practice for samples of the size used in the example, such a criterion is impossible to achieve without excessive *over*fitting. A more appropriate criterion corresponding to an optimum GFI value for a sample of this size is twice the degrees of freedom (Carmines & McIver 1981). Note that with correlational data, standard errors and t values for the parameter estimates in the structural-equation model only approximate the true values and provide little useful information (Jöreskog & Sörbom 1979).

Table 2.2 shows that the most constrained form of each of the models has a very poor fit to the data: χ^2 relative to degrees of freedom is very large (infinitely large in the case of model 1a), and for model 2a the other indices similarly have values suggesting a poor fit. For the single-factor model, the χ^2 of the constrained version (1a) is too large to be calculated. Releasing the constraints on the correlations between the residuals of some of the variables as indicated by the largest modification indices improves the fit, but χ^2 is still six times the degrees of freedom. Clearly the model has a poor fit to the data, which is unlikely to be substantially improved by further adjustments to the model. The alternative two-factor model fares better. Although in the constrained form (2a) the fit is worse, when constraints on some of the residual correlations are removed (model 2b) χ^2 drops to its lowest level but is still as high as three times the degrees of freedom. The model also has the oddity that the loading for test 6, usage, exceeds one.

This type of result, which is fairly common in LISREL, offends the basic principle of the factor model which requires all factor loadings to be less than one. Its existence suggests that the model is inappropriate or still too constrained for the data. Further modifications to the model and relaxation of constraints on the basis of the LISREL diagnostic information might remove the anomalous loading and improve the fit further; but doing much more of this in the absence of strong theoretical justification runs the risk of obtaining a model that fits well simply by capitalizing on chance.

Note that the correlation between the two factors in Figure 2.5 is .85, suggesting a very strong relation between them. Before the advent of confirmatory factor analysis, most psychometricians would have seen this as evidence that the factors are really reflecting the same thing, namely g.

SIMPLEX MODELS

An alternative way of modeling the structure of relationships among the tests is in terms of a simplex, as described in chapter 1. Here we relate each test to the next in a linear sequence in which the strength of relationship between each pair of tests is indicated by a path coefficient or partial standardized regression coefficient. Since none of the tests has perfect reliability, we also include measurement error in the model, producing what is called a "quasi-simplex." Including measurement errors in the model has the effect of correcting the path coefficients for attenuation.

We undertake the fitting of the simplex model to the data in two stages, first for the verbal tests 1–6 and then for the math tests 7 and 8 as well. In stage one we fit a simplex model to the verbal test data with the tests in their original order (model 3); we then see what improvements, if any, can be achieved by reordering the tests in such a way as to produce a pattern of correlations that conforms more closely to the pattern produced by a simplex (model 4). Table 2.3 gives the results of the goodness-of-fit tests, and Figure 2.6 gives the parameter estimates for model 4.

It is clear that model 3 (with the tests in the original order) has a poor fit. Chi-square is eight times the degrees of freedom, and the other indices have poor values. Model 4 fits the data very well, however. The size of χ^2 drops below twice the degrees of freedom, GFI is close to one, and RMS is close to zero.

Clearly a strong simplex exists in the verbal tests. Does this extend to the math tests as well? The next model is formulated on the basis that verbal skills precede mathematical skills, and that the linear sequence can, therefore, be most sensibly extended on to the math tests. Two versions of this model are tested: model 5a is a simple extension of the simplex to include the mathematics tests without any correlations among

Table 2.3
Goodness-of-Fit Statistics for Simplex Models (Verbal Tests)

Model	χ^2	df	GFI	RMS
3	51.52	6	.983	.021
4	9.49	6	.997	.008

Notes:
   Model 3 has variables in their original order (see Table 2.1).
   Model 4 has variable 6 (usage) relocated between variable 2 (comprehension) and variable 3 (spelling).

Figure 2.6
Simplex Model 4

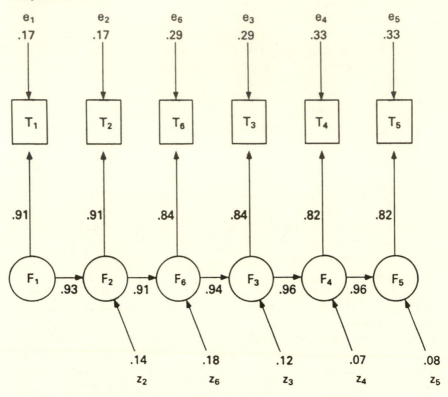

Key: F = test corrected for attenuation, T = test, e = residual measurement error variance,
z = residual variance.

Source: From "Intelligence, fact or artefact: Alternative structures for cognitive abilities" by
J. M. Bynner and D. M. Romney, 1986, *British Journal of Educational Psychology,
56,* p. 19. Copyright 1986 by the British Psychological Society. Reprinted by permission.

residuals; model 5b includes a correlation between residuals for two of
the tests, 6 and 7, as indicated by the LISREL diagnostic information.
Table 2.4 gives the goodness-of-fit test results, and Figure 2.7 gives the
parameter estimates for model 5b.

It is clear that model 5b has a markedly better fit than model 5a, though
nowhere nearly as good a fit as that for the verbal tests alone. The fit is
still an improvement over that for the two-factor model (Figure 2.5), but
model 5b raises theoretical difficulties.

First, the residual correlation estimated by the program turns out to be
negative, a result that is difficult to interpret sensibly. Second, inspection

Table 2.4
Goodness-of-Fit Statistics for Extended-Simplex Models (Verbal and Math Tests)

Model	χ^2	df	GFI	RMS
5a	89.87	15	.976	.025
5b	30.59	15	.991	.012

Notes:
  Model 5a has no correlations between residuals.
  Model 5b releases the constraint on the correlation between the residuals z_7z_6.

of the residual correlations among the tests suggests that substantial residual correlations remain for some tests. The math tests (7 and 8) appear to be more closely related to some of the tests intermediate in the linear sequence than to those at the end; hence large residuals appear in the model for the former two tests.

Initially it was difficult to see what kind of model could embrace these relationships in a way that was both theoretically satisfying and empirically viable. Finally, by considering the likely cognitive development processes involved in the production of the test scores and by testing further through LISREL a range of alternative linkages, we arrived at a model termed, for convenience, a "split simplex." This linked the two math tests directly to the first test in the linear sequence for the verbal tests, vocabulary. So we now had two linear sequences, one for the verbal tests and one for the mathematics tests, both originating from a single skill, vocabulary. Two forms of the model were tested, the first (model 6a) without any residual correlations and the second (model 6b) with residual correlations between test 7 (math concepts) and tests 6 (usage) and 3 (spelling), and also between test 8 (math problems) and test 3 (spelling). Again, indications of the need to include these residual correlations in the model came from the LISREL diagnostic information. This time, as Table 2.5 shows, a very good fit is achieved: for model 6b, the size of χ^2 drops to below twice the degrees of freedom and the GFI and RMS indices both suggest an excellent fit. As Figure 2.8 shows for this model, all of the residual correlations are positive, and all other parameters estimated are readily interpretable in causal terms.

Model 6b clearly matches all our criteria for a good fit and is also an interpretable model. Before placing too much weight on it, however, we need to know how replicable it is. As the Richmond Tests data were

Figure 2.7
Extended-Simplex Model 5b

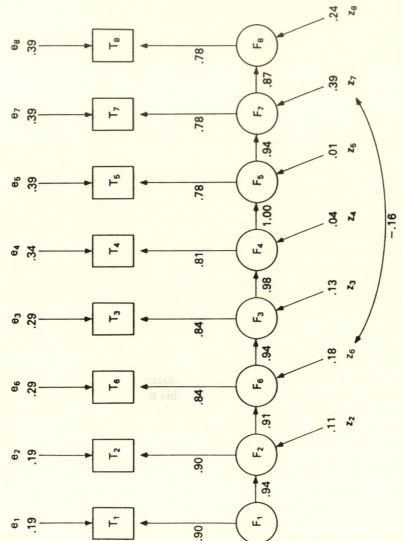

Source: From "Intelligence, fact or artefact: Alternative structures for cognitive abilities" by J. M. Bynner and D.M. Romney, 1986, *British Journal of Educational Psychology, 56,* p. 17. Copyright 1986 by the British Psychological Society. Reprinted by permission.

Table 2.5
Goodness-of-Fit Statistics for Split-Simplex Models (Verbal and Math Tests)

Model	χ^2	df	GFI	RMS
6a	99.62	16	.970	.030
6b	23.26	13	.992	.010

Notes:
Model 6a has no correlations between residuals.
Model 6b releases the constraints on z_7z_6, z_7,z_3, and z_8,z_3.

collected from three cohorts of children in successive years, we were able to check on whether the fit of the model had been achieved more by luck than by good theoretical judgment. Replication across three subsamples of children confirmed our original conclusion; χ^2 varied between 24.89 and 19.43; in no case did it exceed twice the degrees of freedom, and in every replication the GFI was close to one and the RMS close to zero. The only discernible weaknesses in the model were indicated by the modification indices. These pointed to possible additional residual correlations that might improve the fit even further.

ANCHORING THE SIMPLEX

Though we can now be reasonably confident in the representation of the ability tests by a split simplex, use of this model as a guide to educational practice requires a further step. A simplex provides evidence of sequential ordering; if we want to place a causal interpretation on this ordering, however, we need to know in which direction the causal influence is most likely to flow. Figure 2.6 suggests a flow of influence from vocabulary outwards, but the flow could just as easily go in the other direction. Improvement in skill at punctuation, for example, could precede changes in vocabulary. To adjudicate between the two possibilities, we draw on another set of data collected from the Birmingham children.

Before entering the school at the age of eleven, each of the Birmingham children had taken a standard verbal reasoning test (VR). It is reasonable to assume that those tests with the highest correlations with verbal reasoning are closest to it in time and, therefore, causally precede those tests with lower correlations. Table 2.6 shows that the correlations do form a

Figure 2.8
Split-Simplex Model 6b

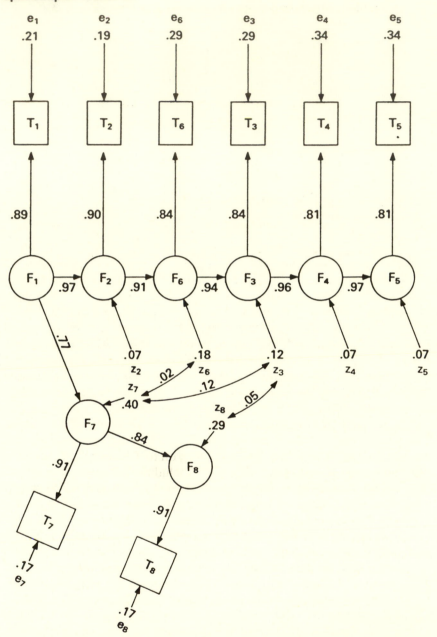

Table 2.6
Correlations Between Verbal Reasoning and Richmond Tests

```
--------------------------

    Richmond Tests       r

--------------------------

    1. Vocabulary        .68

    2. Comprehension     .69

    6. Usage             .62

    3. Spelling          .64

    4. Capitalization    .61

    5. Punctuation       .58

    7. Math concepts     .72

    8. Math problems     .62

--------------------------
```

rank order that supports the causal direction suggested in Figure 2.6. LISREL enables us to test this hypothesis more rigorously by including VR in the model. In effect we "anchor" the split-simplex model (Bynner 1989) by estimating the paths from VR to all the other variables. Initially we formulate the model (7a) with the paths running from VR first to vocabulary and then on to the other variables (see Figure 2.9); next we formulate it (7b) with the paths running from VR first to punctuation and the math problems simultaneously and then on to the other variables (i.e., with the causal directions all reversed). Including VR in the model also allows us to determine to what degree the paths between the variables within the split simplex are reduced in strength when VR is controlled for.

Table 2.7 shows the goodness-of-fit statistics for the two versions of the model, model 7a with VR preceding vocabulary and model 7b with VR preceding the math and the punctuation tests. Table 2.8 gives the model 7a path coefficients from VR to the other variables and the path coefficients between the other variables. For comparison, the path coefficients for the other variables are also shown for the "unanchored" split-simplex model (model 6b).

It is clear that model 7a fits better than model 7b, suggesting that vocabulary has causal priority in both verbal and math sequences. Even more convincing is the relative size of the path coefficients running from VR to each of the tests in the split simplex. These path coefficients tend to

Figure 2.9
Anchored-Simplex Model 7a

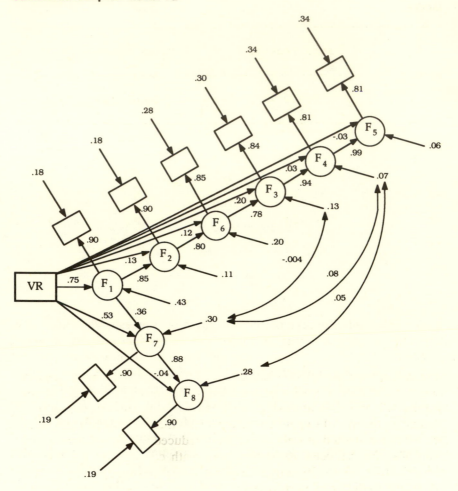

Table 2.7
Goodness-of-Fit Statistics for Anchored-Simplex Models

Model	χ^2	df	GFI	RMS
7a	20.84	13	.996	.008
7b	124.21	13	.927	.044

Table 2.8
Path Coefficients for Split-Simplex Model and Anchored-Simplex Model

Factor	Paths from VR Model 7a	Paths between abilities Model 7a	Model 6b
F1	.75	–	–
F2	.13	.85	.97
F6	.12	.80	.91
F3	.20	.78	.94
F4	.03	.94	.96
F5	-.03	.99	.97
F7	.53	.36	.77
F8	-.04	.88	.84

decrease in size along both sequences, finally ending up with negative values in the case of math problems and punctuation. The effect of controlling VR on the relationships between the tests can also be seen by comparing the model 7a path coefficients with those for the original model 6b. All are sustained at only moderately reduced levels with one exception. The link between vocabulary and math concepts is substantially reduced from .77 to .36, suggesting that verbal reasoning is in itself an important mediator of performance on the math concepts test. But the more interesting result lies in the failure of verbal reasoning overall to "account for" the relations among the tests. VR is the kind of cognitive skill associated with Spearman's *g* factor. There is clearly much more in the generation of the cognitive abilities measured by the Richmond Tests than the exercise of general ability, *g*.

DYNAMIC COGNITIVE DEVELOPMENT

We make no claim that the analysis discussed here is a comprehensive analysis of cognitive abilities; the Richmond Tests of Basic Skills are far too limited for that. What the analysis does is illustrate the value of alternative ways of interpreting correlations among ability-test performances within the structural-equation modeling framework. The customary application of factor models to account for ability test correlation data, though valid to the extent of serving to classify test performances, can be seriously challenged when a different type of causal model is applied to the correlations on which the factor model rests.

The factor model implies that there are underlying latent traits that generate the various abilities measured by the tests. Partialing out the effects of the traits from the correlations may reduce the correlations to zero, but this tells us nothing about the underlying mechanisms involved. Pressure and volume may be perfectly correlated in gases of constant temperature, but no one would model their relationship in terms of an underlying factor. Such physical laws as Boyle's Law express the true functional relationship. Functional relationships give us the guides needed for intervention and change in dynamic systems. Factors as agents of causation rather than as principles of classification lead too easily to a static picture of a genotypic determinacy that places limits on cognitive growth.

This is, of course, the appeal of the alternative split-simplex model for the Richmond Tests. Here we have two linear sequences of abilities in which each ability can be considered to feed the next and in which both sets of abilities ultimately reside in the most fundamental of all cognitive competencies, vocabulary. But vocabulary is itself growing continually, as are all the other skills in response to the education process. The attraction of the model is that it suggests a flow of influence from one skill to the next, so that improvements percolate down and across the sequences in response to the learning process. This is, of course, what every teacher would like to believe occurs, but what theoreticians schooled in factor analysis have tended to dismiss because it is incompatible with their theory.

Such a conception is in line with the ideas of the more developmentally oriented cognitive theorists. Piaget (1983) conceived of cognitive abilities as unfolding through a series of developmental stages. McVicker Hunt (1961) stressed the effect that impoverished learning environments could have in impeding cognitive growth. More recently, Sternberg (1977, 1980, 1985) identified performance on ability tests with the utilization of three distinct types of cognitive components, broadly identified with reasoning, learning, and performance, each interacting with and influencing the other. Feedback ensures constant development of the whole system in response to the educational process. Blockage similarly points to retardation and stagnation. Unlike most of his predecessors in the factor tradition, Sternberg leaves open the question of whether the origins of these components lie primarily in heredity or in the environment. And this perhaps is where the critical issue for educators arises. The use of tests to tap into the state of cognitive processes rather than to control cognitive performance shifts the educational program from selection to diagnosis and facilitation.

TEACHING FOR GROWTH

The alternative educational agendas implied by the two different theoretical positions are easy to see. In factor theory, factors are conceptualized as the causes of abilities; hence, improvements in one ability are unlikely to have much effect on any other ability. Tests therefore are mainly a means of educational selection. They tell the educator what aptitudes the individual has and, therefore, what curriculum is suitable for him or her. Britain's 11+ Examination was premised on this principle and was used to allocate eleven-year-olds to either the academically directed grammar school or the more vocationally oriented secondary modern school. Jensen's massive text *Bias in Mental Testing* (1980) is devoted largely to making the case for such uses.

The alternative split-simplex model leads to a quite different conception of ability and the role of cognitive tests in education. Tests are now perceived not as the means of summatively assessing "potential," but as formative devices for diagnosing strengths and weaknesses in abilities that are themselves continually improving in response to teaching. Identifying the weak links in the process of ability transfer, therefore, becomes as important as teaching the skills themselves. The critical role of vocabulary in the postulated causal chain points to the possible origins of certain children's educational difficulties. Verbally impoverished home environments and family backgrounds, where the language spoken is not the same as the language of instruction at school, may be seen as inhibiting the process of cognitive skill acquisition across the whole curriculum. Too often a child's "educational backwardness" has been seen as something inherent in the child's genetic make-up rather than as a sign of developmental difficulties and a need for remediation that is completely within the scope of education to provide.

The latter view is aligned closely with that of Feuerstein's (1979) prescription for improving cognitive skills in educationally backward children. His "Learning Potential Assessment Device" was designed to maximize the learner's test performance by adapting the conditions of testing and the instructions to match the learner's needs. The success of his approach was shown by the high performances he was able to elicit from children who were incapable of doing standardized intelligence tests. The test also had greater predictive validity than other measures in predicting how the children were likely to perform in other situations. But despite the appeal of Feuerstein's program, the main body of ability testing has stayed firmly with the traditional strategies of assessment, selection, and placement.

Finally we return to a methodological point. Although correlations between test scores may be considerably reduced when the effects of common factors are partialed out, the notion that they all reside basically in the same fixed attribute does not do justice to the rich and complex teaching and learning process that has given rise to them. It cannot be stated strongly enough that the mere evidence of high intercorrelation tells us nothing about its causes.

In the more liberated approach to the study of cognitive abilities, structural-equation modeling is, of course, only a small part of a much larger program of theory development and empirical testing in which the whole range of observational, correlational, and experimental evidence on cognitive performance is brought into play. The requirements of internal and external validity caution against reliance on any single source of evidence to advance the claims of a particular theory. Certainly causal inference can only be most tentatively founded on the evidence of sets of correlations of the kind considered here. What this type of analysis can do is rule out certain kinds of causal explanations and open up alternative theoretical and practical possibilities. Structural-equation modeling proves its value in showing how this may be done.

Chapter 3

Personality: Sequences and Circles

TRADITIONAL MODELS
OF PERSONALITY STRUCTURE

Abilities concern functioning in the performance of tasks; cognitive abilities concern those tasks in the domain of mental or intellectual activity of various kinds. In this chapter we turn to the domain of temperament and feelings: How do we relate to other people? What do we feel about ourselves? In short, what constitutes "personality"? Knowledge of personality can be critical to understanding why a person performs or fails to perform a task or, more globally, in achieving or failing to achieve an ambition. It is also critical to understanding where difficulties in adjustment to new situations and new people lie. Where severe problems occur, the origins may be sought in what clinical psychologists and psychiatrists describe as "personality disorders," maladaptive personal characteristics that precipitate psychological disturbance and breakdown. There is disagreement about whether continuities exist between the "normal" and the "disordered" personality. Psychiatrists working with medical models tend to see the two as quite distinct. Psychologists tend to see the abnormal as no more than an extreme version of the normal—the stance we adopt here. The questions arise, then, as they did with ability: What is personality? How can we most effectively describe it?

The term "personality" is commonly used to describe those enduring traits or patterns of traits believed to underlie an individual's behavior; but there is no agreement on what these traits should be or how many of them there are. There is agreement, however, that an individual's personality reveals itself in his or her outward behavior. Hence we can infer what kind of personality he or she has from the way they generally behave. The concept of personality implies that behavior is *stable* (i.e., it will remain fairly constant over time) and behavior is fairly *consistent* across different situations. Moreover, it is taken for granted that people have different personalities and that they are unique. This does not, of course, preclude the possibility that some people have similar personalities (e.g., identical twins).

When we describe "behavior" as being stable and consistent, we do not mean that it consists merely of specific habitual acts of behavior, for example, biting nails or playing football, but of more enduring traits such as impulsivity, sociability, and so on. It is the possession of these traits that predisposes people to behave in particular ways. Traits are possessed to a greater or lesser extent and may be represented by continuous, relatively independent *dimensions,* with some individuals falling at either end but most falling in between. As we have noted, those individuals with extreme scores on these dimensions may be regarded as having an abnormal personality or personality disorder, but we will discuss this in more detail later.

Traits have been objected to on the grounds that they are *descriptive* rather than *explanatory* terms. To say that a person behaves aggressively because he or she is aggressive does indeed seem like circular reasoning. However, one could make the same argument about the law of gravitation (i.e., things fall because of the force of gravity). The point is that the law of gravitation enables us to make all sorts of verifiable predictions about falling objects. Similarly, knowing an individual's constellation of traits should allow us to predict how this individual will behave in certain circumstances, as distinct from someone else who has a different constellation of traits.

The number of postulated traits is legion (Allport 1931). It has been argued that many of these traits are related to each other and can be grouped together into *clusters* of traits that suggest the existence of broad personality *types* such as extroversion and neuroticism. The notion of personality types goes back to Hippocrates (c. 400 B.C.), who divided all humanity into four basic types: melancholic, choleric, sanguine, and phlegmatic. These terms are still used today with much the same meanings.

Traits are considered to be underlying predispositions that are not directly observable but that make us prone to behave in certain ways, much as abilities are considered to underlie our performance on cognitive and psychomotor tasks. Consequently, traits are also identified with latent variables or factors. Evidence for the existence of these traits has typically come in the past from factor analysis. The number of traits that make up personality and the relationships of these traits to each other constitute the *structure* of personality.

Personality testing took over the techniques of research on intelligence and applied them to the task of unraveling the structure of personality. The most common form of a personality test is the questionnaire that measures the respondents' views of themselves. The limitation to this approach is that self-report is subject to inaccuracies and distortions. The other main technique for assessing personality is to have observers rate other people's behavior, usually on standard sets of rating scales. Again, this method is not foolproof because observers can also make mistakes.

SITUATIONISM AND INTERACTIONISM

Although personality will to some extent determine behavior, situational factors also have to be taken into account. In fact, behaviorists tend to attach more importance to the situation than to personality as a determinant of behavior. Mischel (1968), for instance, argued that personality accounted for very little of the variance in behavior compared to the specific situation in which the behavior occurred. Other psychologists, the most notable being Bowers (1973) and Endler and Magnusson (1976), have argued that it is not so much personality or the situation that determines an individual's behavior but rather the *interaction* between them. However, this controversy is not central to the structure of personal characteristics and the traits that underlie them.

SINGLE-TRAIT VERSUS MULTITRAIT THEORIES

Single-trait theories are concerned with the part played by one particular trait in the determination of behavior. Multitrait theories are concerned with two or more traits. Examples of single traits that have received considerable attention are *authoritarianism* (Adorno, Frenkel-Brunswick, Levinson, & Sanford 1950), *achievement motivation* (Mc-Clelland, Atkinson, Clark, & Lowell 1953), *repression-sensitization* or *alexithymia* (Byrne 1964), *field dependence–independence* (Witkin et al. 1972), and *locus of control* (Rotter 1966). The current popularity of single-trait theories lies in the relative ease of assessment and manipulation of single traits. However, this approach to personality fails to address the full complexity of personality in the way attempted by multitrait theorists. Eysenck, Cattell, and Norman are the best known of these and will be considered next. Other personality theorists worthy of note but who will not be discussed here are Guilford (1975) and Murray (1938). Guilford's work on personality, which relied on a multifactor description, has had much less impact than his work on intelligence (see chapter 2). Murray's theory was more concerned with "needs" than with traits.

EYSENCK'S PERSONALITY THEORY

Eysenck was one of the first theorists to apply the methods of factor analysis to the study of personality. Starting from Jung's theory in which people were classified as either outgoing (extroverted) or inward-looking (introverted), Eysenck's factorial approach first led him to the conclusion that only two underlying general factors were necessary to account for individual differences in personality. One of these was a bipolar factor corresponding to Jung's extroversion/introversion concept, and the other was a unipolar factor, neuroticism or emotional instability. Extroversion is associated with sociability and impulsiveness, in contrast to introversion, which is associated with being withdrawn, solitary, and restrained. Neuroticism is associated with being highly strung, tense, and anxious, stability with being calm and relaxed. These two dimensions are unrelated to each other, and together they yield four quadrants that correspond to the four types defined by Hippocrates (see Figure 3.1).

Eysenck's theory was primarily directed at explaining personality disorders and breakdowns. He applied his two-dimensional personality theory to the classification of psychiatric patients, hypothesizing that neurotics who were introverted would be diagnosed as anxious, depressed, or obsessional, whereas neurotics who were extroverted would be diagnosed as hysterical or psychopathic. An empirical study (Eysenck 1944) that involved rating 700 neurotic soldiers and then performing a factor analysis on these ratings supported the existence of these two independent dimensions. Moreover, as he postulated, the neuroticism factor represented items concerned with the severity of the disorder, whereas the introversion/extroversion bipolar factor discriminated between the two major forms of neurosis—anxiety and hysteria—as they were then named. The Eysenck Personality Inventory (EPI) is the scale currently used to determine people's location on these two dimensions (H. J. Eysenck & S. B. G. Eysenck 1964).

Figure 3.1
Hypothesized Human Personality Dimensions Encompassing Earlier Conceptualizations

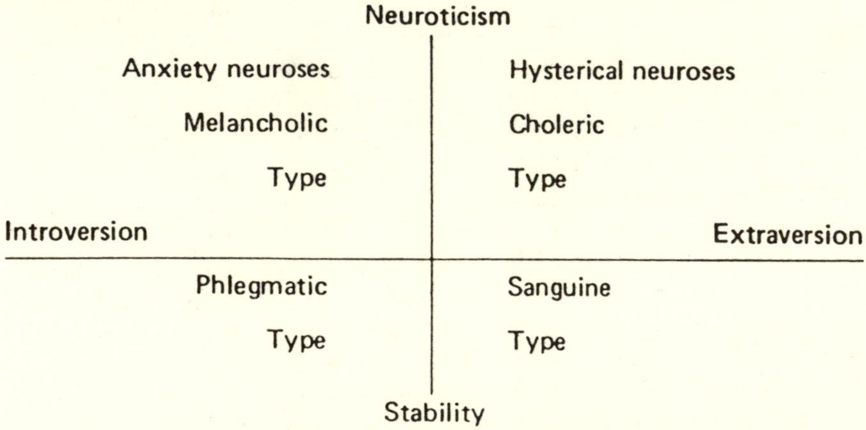

                                    Neuroticism

        Anxiety neuroses | Hysterical neuroses

            Melancholic | Choleric

                    Type | Type

Introversion | Extraversion
_____|_____
            Phlegmatic | Sanguine

                    Type | Type

                                  |
                                Stability

Source: From *The Construction of Personality: An Introduction* (2nd ed., p. 48) by S. E. Hampson, 1988, London: Routledge. Copyright 1982, 1988 by Sarah E. Hampson. Reprinted by permission.

Afterwards, Eysenck expanded his theory of personality structure to include a third dimension, psychoticism, which was independent of both neuroticism and extroversion and which indicated proneness to psychotic breakdown (S. B. G. Eysenck & H. J. Eysenck 1968). However, the Eysencks found that psychoticism and neuroticism were not completely independent and that criminals tended to score high on psychoticism. A scale was devised to measure all three personality dimensions, known as the Eysenck Personality Questionnaire (H. J. Eysenck & S. B. G. Eysenck 1975).

Because any personality theory that reduces the whole of human behavior, with all its complexities, to a mere three factors might invite skepticism, Eysenck adopted a hierarchical model of personality, much like the hierarchical model of intelligence discussed in chapter 2. At the bottom of the hierarchy are *specific actions,* such as reading a newspaper or answering a question. At the next level come *habitual responses;* for example, being friendly to strangers, enjoying parties, and so on. On top of this level come the actual *traits* that we have been discussing, such as sociability. At the top of the hierarchy lie the personality *types,* such as extroversion, that are composed of related traits (see Figure 3.2).

Figure 3.2
Eysenck's Hierarchical Model of Personality

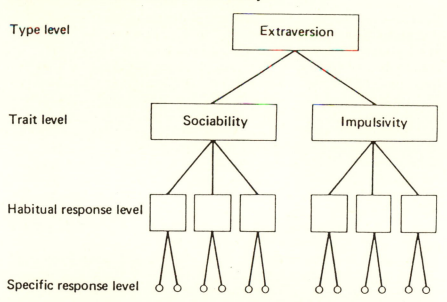

Source: From *The Psychology of Politics* (p. 112) by H. J. Eysenck, 1957, London: Routledge & Kegan Paul. Copyright 1957 by Routledge & Kegan Paul. Reprinted by permission.

FIRST-ORDER AND SECOND-ORDER FACTORS

This hierarchical model of personality structure is identical in form to the hierarchical models of intelligence that we reviewed in chapter 2. The habitual- and specific-response levels in the hierarchy correspond to the items found in personality inventories and rating scales. These items correlate with each other, and when the matrix of correlations of items is factor analyzed, factors or traits emerge to account for them. The traits themselves, however, are also intercorrelated, and the matrix of correlations of traits can then be factor analyzed to give rise to "higher order" factors or types. Hence, trait levels are designated as *first-order factors* and type levels as *second-order factors*.

CATTELL'S PERSONALITY THEORY

Cattell (1943) reasoned that the structure of personality could be identified from the adjectives used in everyday language to describe personality. Allport and Odbert (1936) had surveyed the English language and found about 4,500 adjectives that specifically describe personality. Cattell managed to reduce this huge number, on the basis of their semantic similarity, to 171 groups of synonyms. Bipolar rating scales were constructed to represent these groups of synonyms; from their intercorrelations in a peer-rating study, he identified thirty-five clusters that he then used as a basis for constructing further rating scales. He subsequently found, after performing a series of factor-analytic studies, that first twelve (Cattell 1945) and then sixteen *personality factors* (Cattell 1957) were necessary to account for the correlations between the rating scales representing the thirty-five clusters. The sixteen factors, and the traits they reflect, are listed in Table 3.1. They can be measured by means of the Sixteen Personality Factors Questionnaire (Cattell, Eber, & Tatsuoka 1970).

How is it, one may ask, that Cattell arrived at sixteen personality factors when Eysenck discovered only three? As we saw in the previous chapter, the answer lies in part with the *indeterminacy* of factor analysis. We do not know in advance, for instance, how many factors to extract, how much of the variance is common and how much is specific, and whether or not the factors are related to each other. Eysenck, in the tradition of Spearman, assumed that a few unrelated (i.e., "orthogonal") factors were all that were necessary to explain personality structure, whereas Cattell, following in the footsteps of Thurstone and adopting the "simple structure" approach, believed that the complexities of personality could only be described adequately by sixteen oblique factors. The correlations among the sixteen factors raised the possibility of whether deeper factors could be considered to underlie even them. It is noteworthy that, when the sixteen factors were themselves factor analyzed, two

Table 3.1
Descriptions of Traits Measured by the Sixteen Personality Factors
Questionnaire

Factor	Description
A	*Reserved*, detached, critical, cool, versus *Outgoing*, warmhearted, easy-going, participating.
B	*Less intelligent*, concrete-thinking, versus *More intelligent*, abstract-thinking, bright.
C	*Affected by feelings*, emotionally less stable, easily upset, versus *Emotionally stable*, faces reality, calm, mature.
E	*Humble*, mild, accommodating, conforming, versus *Assertive*, independent, aggressive, stubborn.
F	*Sober*, prudent, serious, taciturn, versus *Happy-go-lucky*, impulsively lively, gay, enthusiastic.
G	*Expedient*, evades rules, feels few obligations, versus *Conscientious*, persevering, staid, rule-bound.
H	*Shy*, restrained, diffident, timid, versus *Venturesome*, socially-bold, uninhibited, spontaneous.
I	*Tough-Minded*, self-reliant, realistic, no-nonsense, versus *Tender-Minded*, dependent, overprotected, sensitive.
L	*Trusting*, adaptable, free of jealousy, easy to get on with, versus *Suspicious*, self-opinionated, hard to fool.
M	*Practical*, careful, conventional, proper, versus *Imaginative*, wrapped up in inner urgencies, careless of practical matters, bohemian.
N	*Forthright*, natural, artless, sentimental, versus *Shrewd*, calculating, worldly, penetrating.
O	*Placid*, self-assured, confident, serene, versus *Apprehensive*, worrying, depressive, troubled.
Q_1	*Conservative*, respecting, established ideas, versus *Experimenting*, critical, liberal, analytical, free thinking.
Q_2	*Group-Dependent*, a "joiner," and sound follower, versus *Self-Sufficient*, prefers own decisions, resourceful.
Q_3	*Undisciplined*, Self-Conflict, careless of protocol, versus *Controlled*, socially precise, following self-image.
Q_4	*Relaxed*, tranquil, torpid, unfrustrated, versus *Tense*, frustrated, driven, overwrought.

of the second-order factors that emerged appeared very similar to extroversion and neuroticism. More recently, a compromise between Eysenck's "too few" factors and Cattell's "too many" factors seems to have been reached with the theory that *five* personality factors are needed to describe the structure of personality. These five factors have come to be known as the "Big Five."

THE BIG FIVE DIMENSIONS OF PERSONALITY

Fiske (1949), obtaining both self-ratings and peer ratings from graduate students by means of twenty-two bipolar scales chosen from Cattell's original thirty-five clusters, found nothing more complex than a five-factor solution. Later, Tupes and Christal (1958) replicated this study on twenty of the twenty-two clusters selected by Fiske by investigating the factor structure of peer ratings of servicemen. The five factors to emerge were identified as *surgency, agreeableness, conscientiousness, emotional stability,* and *culture*.

While Fiske (1949) may have been the first to discover the Big Five, and Tupes and Christal (1958) the first to identify them, most of the systematic work on them was done by Norman (1963), thus the Big Five were known initially as the Norman Five. Norman replicated earlier findings on university students and provided a cogent justification for the five-factor solution. Wiggins and Trapnell (in press) describe Norman's contribution as follows:

a milestone in the historical development of the five-factor model because it provided (1) a clear statement of the rationale and procedures for developing a well-structured taxonomy of personality attributes; (2) psychometric criticisms of Cattell's earlier factorial work and an advocation of analytic orthogonal rotation; (3) an analytic comparison of the generalizability of the five-factor solution within an appropriate experimental design; and (4) a call for the development of self-report measures of the five-factors, using peer ratings as criteria.

Table 3.2 shows the scales that are associated with each of the five factors.

Goldberg (1981) asked the question: How *robust* is the five-factor solution to procedural variations? To answer this question, he tested every kind of available popular factor-analysis program together with different types of rotation. He found the same five factors and similar factor loadings each time. On the basis of this research using different algorithms and on the basis of other research comparing (1) peer reports with self-reports and (2) various kinds of rating scales, he came to this important conclusion: "Whether the data come from self-reports or from descriptions of other people, whether based on one kind of rating scale or another, no

Table 3.2
The Five Factors Representing the Twenty Peer Nomination Scales

Factor Name	Scale Labels
Extroversion	talkative-silent frank, open-secretive adventurous-cautious sociable-reclusive
Agreeableness	good-natured-irritable not jealous-jealous mild, gentle-headstrong cooperative-negativistic
Conscientious	fussy, tidy-careless responsible-undependable scrupulous-unscrupulous persevering-quitting, fickle
Emotional stability	poised-nervous, tense calm-anxious composed-excitable non-hypochondriacal-hypochondriacal
Culture	artistically sensitive-artistically insensitive intellectual-unreflective, narrow polished, refined-crude, boorish imaginative-simple, direct

matter what the method for factor extraction or rotation, the results are much the same" (160–61).

Goldberg also tried to integrate other theoretical formulations of personality structure into the five-factor framework, including the views of Cattell (1957) and Eysenck (1970). In a recent review of the five-factor model, Digman (1990) has extended this integration to cover other formulations of personality structure that have been proposed since Goldberg's attempt a decade ago (see Table 3.3). It should be noted that extroversion is regarded as being synonymous with surgency, and neuroticism with emotional (in)stability. Eysenck's psychoticism factor is perceived to be a blend of (dis)agreeableness and (lack of) conscientiousness. It should also be noted that agreeableness is interpreted by some researchers as "friendliness" or "likeability," and culture is interpreted by

Table 3.3
The Five Robust Dimensions of Personality from Fiske (1949) to the Present

Author	I	II	III	IV	V
Fiske (1949)	social adaptability	conformity	will to achieve*	emotional control	inquiring intellect
Eysenck (1970)	extraversion	------ P s y c h o t i c i s m ----		neuroticism	
Tupes & Christal (1961)	surgency	agreeableness	dependability	emotionality	culture
Norman (1963)	surgency	agreeableness	conscientiousness	emotional	culture
Borgatta (1964)	assertiveness	likeability	task interest	emotionality	intelligence
Cattell (1957)	exvia	cortertia	superego strength	anxiety	intelligence
Guilford (1975)	social activity	paranoid disposition	thinking introversion	emotional stability	
Digman (1988)	extraversion	friendly compliance	will to achieve	neuroticism	intellect
Hogan (1986)	sociability & ambition	likeability	prudence	adjustment	intellectance
Costa & McCrae (1985)	extraversion	agreeableness	conscientiousness	neuroticism	openness
Peabody & Goldberg (1989)	power	love	work	affect	intellect
Buss & Plomin (1984)	activity	sociability	impulsivity	emotionality	
Tellegen (1985)	positive emotionality		constraint	negative emotionality	
Lorr (1986)	interpersonal involvement	level of socialization	self-control	emotional stability	independent

* Not in the original analysis but noted in a re-analysis by Digman and Takenoto-Chock (1981)

some as "intellect" and by others as "openness to experience." Costa and McCrae (1985) have devised a neuroticism, extroversion, openness personality inventory (NEO-PI), tailor-made to measure the five-factor model. The evidence in favor of the Big Five is very impressive, though much of the earlier work is based on studies of university students rather than the general population. However, the universality of the Big Five cannot be explained by the limited nature of the samples tested to date. The Big Five have now been identified in rating studies of children (Digman & Inouye 1986) and of adults (McCrae & Costa 1985).

THE CIRCUMPLEX MODEL
OF INTERPERSONAL BEHAVIOR

Factors define a multidimensional space in which all of the original variables from which the factors were derived can be located. Relations between the variables in this space open up a different perspective on personality structure. Inspired by a personality theory based on the views of two psychotherapists, Horney (1937) and Sullivan (1953), Leary (1957) was probably the first to suggest that normal personality traits, such as "rebelliousness," "competitiveness," "conformity," and "collaboration," can be located on a circle in a two-dimensional space with traits on opposite sides of the circle forming bipolar contrasts; for example, rebellious-conforming, competitive-collaborative. Traits opposite each other on the circle have maximal negative correlations; traits perpendicular to each other are uncorrelated; positive correlations are maximal between those traits that are close together and decrease as they approach a perpendicular relationship. The original Leary model is shown in Figure 3.3. Note that the more extreme or intense forms of the traits are located closer to the circumference whereas the milder forms are closer to the center.

This circular arrangement of the traits in a two-dimensional space is a function of the location of the traits themselves on either side of the two bipolar factors that form the space; the midpoint of the factors lies at the center of the circle, and the extreme forms of the traits fall on the periphery of the circle. In Leary's model, there are eight bipolar factors, but the variant of his model proposed by Wiggins (1982) has half that number. As these factors intercorrelate, they can be reduced via factor analysis to the two independent second-order factors in which the circumplex is located. These second-order factors are often referred to as affiliation (the horizontal axis) and power (the vertical axis). Affiliation represents a hostile-friendly dimension, and power represents a dominant-submissive dimension. This circle of personality traits with first- and second-order factors is equivalent to a hierarchy of traits. The parallelism between the circumplex and hierarchical factor models reflects the parallelism between the

Figure 3.3
Classification of Interpersonal Behavior into Sixteen Varieties

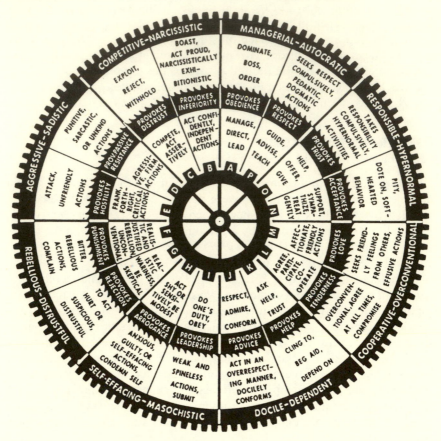

The inner circle represents adaptive forms of the behavior, the middle circle the behavior it tends to evoke in others, and the next circle the rigid or maladaptive forms.

Source: From *Interpersonal Diagnosis of Personality: A Functional Theory and Methodology for Personality Evaluation* (p. 65) by T. F. Leary, 1957, New York: Ronald Press. Copyright 1957 by Ronald Press. Reprinted by permission.

radex and hierarchical factor models alluded to in the previous chapter on abilities (cf. Snow, Kyllonen, & Marshalek 1984).

It should be emphasized that, in this model and all its variants, the traits were chosen to describe *interpersonal* behavior, reflecting how people interact socially with each other. The Interpersonal Check List (ICL; LaForge 1977) can be used to provide either self-ratings of interpersonal behavior or the ratings of others. Scores are calculated for sixteen interpersonal behaviors and the results plotted on a circular chart.

The circumplex model seems particularly well suited to represent the prototypic approach to personality classification (Cantor, Smith, French, & Mezzich 1980). This approach is based on the empirical research on human categorization by Rosch (1978), who argued that categories have fuzzy rather than sharply defined boundaries and that, although there exist "prototypes" that epitomize the categories, these are surrounded by other less clear-cut cases whose membership in the category is more equivocal, the probability of membership depending on their degree of resemblance to the prototype. As we start to move round the circle either clockwise or counterclockwise away from a given trait, the nature of that particular trait changes gradually and continuously, becoming more and more like its neighboring trait. This model of personality traits contrasts with the categorical notion of traits as discrete phenomena which are qualitatively different from each other, and the dimensional approach which emphasizes the distinctiveness of latent traits identified with factors.

THE CIRCUMPLEX PATTERN OF CORRELATIONS

As we saw in the previous chapter, the general circumplex model was first proposed by Guttman (1954) for variables that form a circular order. The "circulant" correlational pattern identifying such an ordering for seven variables is shown in Table 3.4. A circulant matrix is an idealized matrix of the pattern of intercorrelations that should theoretically occur in the population from which the sample is drawn. The restriction $r_1 > r_2 > r_3 > r_4$ defines the matrix as one in which the correlations decrease from the principal diagonal to a minimum value and then increase again as the corners are approached. The correlations along the first off-diagonal and the one in the lower-left corner all have the same value (r_1). Similarly, the correlations between adjacent variables (1 and 2, 2 and 3, etc.) are equal to one another. Of course, correlation matrices derived from samples can only approximate such a perfect arrangement. This strict pattern is assumed to exist only in populations. As we shall see later, using SEM, we can test how well the sample (circumplex) matrix corresponds to the population (circulant) matrix.

PERSONALITY DISORDERS

When individuals hold a trait to an extreme degree and are inflexible in their behavior, they can be described as having a *personality disorder*. The essence of a personality disorder is the manifestation of intense and rigid personality traits. As a consequence, personality-disordered individuals behave in a maladaptive fashion, so they experience significantly impaired social and occupational functioning or subjective distress. As

Table 3.4
Representation of a Circumplex-Correlation Matrix

	1	2	3	4	5	6
1	1					
2	r_1	1				
3	r_2	r_1	1			
4	r_3	r_2	r_1	1		
5	r_4	r_3	r_2	r_1	1	
6	r_3	r_4	r_3	r_2	r_1	1
7	r_2	r_3	r_4	r_3	r_2	r_1

Note: $r_1 > r_2 > r_3 > r_4$.

Skodol (1989) puts it: "The important features that distinguish pathological personality traits from normal are their inflexibility and maladap-
tiveness. Inflexibility is indicated by a narrow repertoire of responses that
are repeated even when the situation calls for an alternate behavior or in
the face of clear evidence that a behavior is inappropriate or not working"
(p. 385).

Psychiatrists have differentiated as many as eleven different personality
disorders in the revised *Diagnostic and Statistical Manual of Mental
Disorders* (DSM-III-R; American Psychiatric Press, 1987), which is the
official diagnostic manual of the American Psychiatric Association. Each
of the personality disorders is diagnosed on clinical grounds according to
the manifestation of particular traits which are stipulated in the manual.
Until recently, personality disorders were of interest primarily to therapists involved in long-term, psychodynamic therapy; they have since at-
tracted the attention of interpersonal and cognitive therapists as well as
diagnosticians and researchers.

Taking a further step, psychiatrists have subdivided the personality disorders into three clusters according to the most prominent traits held in common. Thus cluster A is composed of paranoid, schizoid, and schizotypal personality disorders, in which individuals often appear as odd or eccentric; cluster B encompasses antisocial, borderline, histrionic, and narcissistic personality disorders, in which individuals appear emotional, theatrical, or erratic; and cluster C comprises avoidant, dependent, obsessive-compulsive, and passive-aggressive personality disorders where individuals often appear anxious or fearful. It is worth pointing out that the disorders in cluster A tend to be related to Eysenck's psychoticism dimension, disorders in cluster B to his extroversion dimension, and disorders in cluster C to his neuroticism dimension.

In addition to the eleven official personality disorders, there are two more that have been proposed and that are waiting to be validated; namely, sadistic personality disorder and self-defeating personality disorder. Widiger and Frances (1985) state: "Each personality disorder has a characteristic and dysfunctional personality style that is often the central feature of the disorder" (620). Furthermore, "the abnormal person, rather than possessing the flexibility of the normal individual to use the broad range of interpersonal behaviors warranted by social situations, is locked into a rigid and extreme use of limited classes of personal action" (Kiesler 1986, 572).

An empirical study conducted recently by Sim and Romney (1990) tested the hypotheses that individuals with personality disorders behave in a more extreme or "intense" manner and exhibit more rigid interpersonal behavior than normal individuals. A clinical sample of ninety patients diagnosed by psychiatrists as personality-disordered and a control group of ninety-seven university students were given the Interpersonal Check List (ICL). Both groups were rated on the ICL by individuals who had an opportunity to interact with them for a brief period of time. The results showed that individuals with personality disorders had higher-intensity scores than the normal controls; that is, their traits were located further away from the center of the circle (intensity) and tended to be restricted to the same narrow area of the circle (rigidity). Thus both of the hypotheses were supported. Similar findings have been reported in normal subjects by Wiggins, Phillips, and Trapnell (1989).

PERSONALITY DISORDERS AND THE CIRCUMPLEX

If personality disorders are no more than extreme versions of personality traits, then the factor and circumplex models of personality traits should also apply to them. As we have already stated, personality disorders can be regarded as exaggerations of normal personality traits so that paranoid personality disorder, for instance, can be perceived as the cold-quarrelsome personality trait taken to its extreme. Wiggins (1982) applied the circumplex model to DSM-III personality disorders. He selected seven of the DSM-III personality disorders, added hypomanic personality disorder (which is now considered by psychiatrists to be a transient *state* rather than a lasting personality disorder), and suggested how they could be arranged around a circle together with their corresponding personality traits, as shown in Figure 3.4.

Not everyone agrees with Wiggins's (1982) circular formulation. In particular, controversy exists regarding the placement of compulsive personality disorder. Whereas Wiggins placed compulsive at the dominant end of the dominance-submission dimension, Kiesler (1983) placed it at the submissive end. On the other hand, Widiger, Trull, Hurt, Clarkin, and Frances (1987) have placed it at the center of this dimension, arguing that compulsive personality disorder contains elements of both dominance

Figure 3.4
Wiggins's (1982) Interpersonal Types (outside Perimeter) and
Corresponding Diagnoses (inside Perimeter)

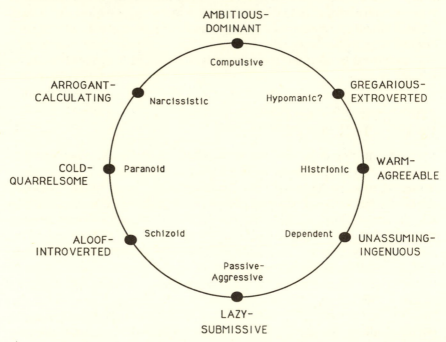

Source: Adapted from "Structural Approaches to Classification" by R. K. Blashfield, 1986, in T. Millon and G. L. Klerman (Eds.), *Contemporary Directions in Psychopathology: Toward the DSM-IV* (p. 389). Copyright 1986 by the Guilford Press. Reprinted by permission.

and submission. Frances and Widiger (1986) pointed out in an earlier paper that a disorder with a strong cognitive component such as compulsive personality disorder is unlikely to conform with a circular pattern defined by affiliation and power; there is empirical evidence from exploratory factor analysis that this disorder taps a separate dimension (Blashfield, Sprock, Pinkston, & Hodgin 1985).

Wiggins (1982) did not attempt to place all known personality disorders on the interpersonal circle because for some the primary deficit is not interpersonal in nature. The interpersonal circle is defined by only two dimensions, and, as we have already seen, at least five dimensions seem necessary to cover the whole gamut of personality traits. The question then arises, Which personality disorders actually do fit on the circle?

Given that different circular arrangements have been postulated, this question is best answered by a structural-equation model that allows *confirmatory* factor analyses (CFA). CFA can confirm the goodness-of-fit of this model to the matrix of correlations by reconstructing a circumplex patterning of correlations from the model and testing how well it coincides with the original correlation matrix. Another advantage of CFA is its capacity to correct for attenuation or error of measurement in order to represent the properties of measurement more precisely in the model. SEM is therefore technically far superior to the traditional approach exemplified by exploratory factor analysis (EFA), which is the method usually employed to identify the principal axes on which the circumplex is based.

STRUCTURAL-EQUATION MODELING
OF THE CIRCUMPLEX

Jöreskog (1974) describes the fitting of a circumplex to ability test data using ACOVS, a precursor of the LISREL program. If we omit hypomanic personality disorder from the eight personality disorders around the circle, because it is not recognized as a personality disorder in DSM-III, the circumplex can be conceptualized in terms of seven underlying orthogonal factors representing the "pure forms" or prototypes of the personality disorders. The fuzziness or overlap among the manifest personality disorder traits does not exist among these factors. Each factor is assumed to load on four of the adjacent variables as shown in Table 3.5 (Cudeck 1986). Thus, the first variable has loadings on factors I, II, III, and IV; the second factor on variables factors II, III, IV, V, and so forth. Factor loadings designated by the same numbers (1, 2, 3, or 4) are constrained to be equal. Note also that each variable shares three factors in common with its neighboring variable. As Cudeck (1986) explains, however, LISREL is not able for technical reasons to accommodate negative correlations in a circumplex matrix. Bentler's (1985) EQS program does

Table 3.5
Representation of a Circulant-Factor Matrix

FACTORS							
Variables	**I**	**II**	**III**	**IV**	**V**	**VI**	**VII**
Paranoid	1	2	3	4	0	0	0
Schizoid	0	1	2	3	4	0	0
Passive-aggressive	0	0	1	2	3	4	0
Dependent	0	0	0	1	2	3	4
Histrionic	4	0	0	0	1	2	3
Compulsive	3	4	0	0	0	1	2
Narcissistic	2	3	4	0	0	0	1

not suffer from this disadvantage. We therefore decided to use EQS to test the fit of a series of circumplex models to correlation matrices of DSM-III personality disorders (Romney & Bynner 1989) reported by Kass, Skodol, Charles, Spitzer, and Williams (1985) and by Hyler and Lyons (1988) with factors (corresponding to the number of variables) linking sets of adjacent variables to the postulated circumplex as described earlier. Two forms of each model are applied: the first without measurement error in the variables (model a) and the second with measurement error (model b). Goodness-of-fit indices express the extent to which the correlation matrix implied by the circumplex model matches the obtained correlation matrix. In EQS these include χ^2, a nonnormed goodness-of-fit index adjusted for degrees of freedom (*NNFI*), and the average absolute standardized residual correlation (AASR). In a model with a good fit, χ^2 will be small relative to degrees of freedom and the probability (p) will be high. Similarly, NNFI will be close to one and AASR close to zero.

KASS AND COLLEAGUES (1985)

In this study, twenty-three psychiatry residents and twelve psychology residents who had received training and supervised practice in making DSM-III diagnoses assessed 609 (mainly working lower-class) outpatients for personality disorder using a 4-point rating scale. The residents were required to rate patients on each of the eleven personality disorders according to whether each patient exhibited (1) none or very few traits, (2) some traits, (3) almost meets DSM-III criteria, and (4) meets DSM-III criteria. An EFA of the correlations between these disorders resulted in four major factors which accounted for 59 percent of the variance in the correlation matrix. The first three factors corresponded to the three clusters of personality disorders (A, B, and C) mentioned earlier; the last factor was reserved for compulsive disorder alone.

This model was tested under two conditions, using the generalized least-squares method, which was the method used by Cudeck (1986). In the first condition (model a), the error variances were fixed at zero in order to test Wiggins's model; and in the second condition (model b), the error variances were set free (i.e., allowed to vary). In both conditions, the variance of factor I was set at unity in order to anchor the metric (Jöreskog 1974, 90).

The first model that was tested replicated Wiggins's model and was designated model 1a. However, Wiggins (1982) had proposed that "hypomanic personality disorder" be included in the eight personality disorders surrounding the circle; this particular disorder could not be included in the analysis, however, because it is not part of the DSM-III classification and was not used by Kass and his colleagues. The fit indices for his model (minus hypomanic personality disorder) are given in Table 3.6 (see model 1a). With the error variances set free (model 1b), however, the iterative estimates of the parameters failed to converge, indicating a very poor fit to the data.

Because compulsive personality disorder has been found to be the "odd man out" in other studies, the matrix was reanalyzed with this variable omitted. But this second model (both 2a and 2b) was also inappropriate, either because the variances of certain factors were constrained at zero (by the computer program) or because of a failure of the iterative process. A third model was tried, with the factors preloaded on *three* instead of four variables. Model 3a was a slight improvement over model 1a, but model 3b was clearly inappropriate. A further examination of the correlation matrix revealed that passive-aggressive personality disorder did not fit the circumplex pattern, so passive-aggressive disorder was consequently discarded and the data reanalyzed without it. The goodness-of-fit indices for models 4a and 4b are given in Table 3.6. They indicate that model 4b, comprising just five of the DSM-III disorders

Table 3.6
Goodness-of-Fit Values for Circumplex Models

1985 data

Model	χ^2	df	NNFI	AASR
1a	130.62	18	.958	.089
1b	–	–	–	–
4a	37.60	8	.983	.055
4b	7.59	3	.993	.021

1988 data

1a	113.62	18	.955	.096
1b	72.01	11	.953	.086
4a	46.06	8	.971	.100
4b	6.74	3	.992	.029

(paranoid, schizoid, dependent, histrionic, and narcissistic), fits the data very well.

HYLER AND LYONS (1988)

This study was a replication of the previous study, except that the ratings were made by a nationwide sample of 287 psychiatrists and the usable sample of 358 patients was predominantly middle-class. The ratings were intercorrelated and subjected to an EFA. The same four factors identified by Kass and his colleagues emerged from this analysis.

The series of four circumplex models that we tested in the previous study were tested again in this study. The fit indices for the corresponding models (1 and 4) are given in Table 3.6. The last model (4b), like its counterpart the study by Kass and his colleagues, provides a very good fit, far better than any of the others.

A FIVE-VARIABLE INTERPERSONAL CIRCUMPLEX?

For the two clinical samples, a clear picture emerges. A circular pattern (as shown in Figure 3.5) is formed by five disorders: paranoid, schizoid,

Figure 3.5
A Five- or Six-Variable Circumplex Model of Personality Disorders

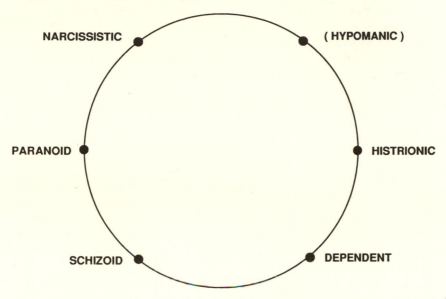

Source: From "Evaluation of a Circumplex Model of DSM-III Personality Disorders" by D. M. Romney and J. M. Bynner, 1989, *Journal of Research in Personality, 23,* p. 534. Copyright 1989 by Academic Press, Inc. Reprinted by permission.

dependent, histrionic, and narcissistic disorders. These comprise the seven personality disorders that Wiggins originally included alongside hypomanic, minus compulsive and passive-aggressive disorders. It is noteworthy that the latter form opposite poles in Wiggins's model; hence, the exclusion of both of them makes logical sense. We have already referred to Frances and Widiger (1986). They criticized the placement of compulsive personality on the interpersonal circle; because of its strong cognitive component, it is unlikely to have an unambiguous location in the interpersonal space defined by affiliation and power. In other words, we could have *predicted* that compulsive personality disorder would not fit comfortably on the circle. And although passive-aggressive personality disorder was not included in their criticism, our analysis suggests that this disorder too may have a possible cognitive component that has not been adequately recognized.

It is also noteworthy that in this circumplex we find the gap identified by Wiggins, a gap resulting from the omission of hypomania from the DSM-III classification. The pole opposite schizoid on the circle would appear to fit the hypomanic description, which suggests that this disorder should be recognized in the prospective DSM-IV not only as a state but also as a trait. Currently, disagreement exists among nosologists over this issue (Widiger, Frances, Spitzer, & Williams 1988). There is, however, additional evidence from the Sim and Romney (1990) study suggesting that hypomania should occupy the top-right quadrant of the interpersonal circle. As with schizoid, histrionic, and compulsive personality disorders, hypomanic personality disorder might be viewed as a predisposition to the corresponding DSM-III disorder (i.e., mania). But this assumption remains to be tested.

Earlier we mentioned that the personality disorders were clustered *a priori* in DSM-III-R into three clusters (A, B, or C), according to the most salient traits held in common. The arrangement of the five disorders in Figure 3.5 is consistent with this clustering: paranoid and schizoid are adjacent (cf. cluster A), and so are narcissistic and histrionic (cf. cluster B), while dependent stays by itself (cf. cluster C). This means that the circular arrangement of the five interpersonal disorders is compatible with their clustering in DSM-III-R.

What about the other personality disorders excluded from Wiggins's model and similarly excluded from our analysis? The structure of their relations to each other and to compulsive and passive-aggressive personality disorders is what we investigated next (Romney & Bynner, 1992).

A SIMPLEX MODEL OF FIVE OTHER
PERSONALITY DISORDERS

Support for omitting some of the personality disorders from the circle is provided by Widiger and Frances (1985), who stated that "the interpersonal circle might fail to adequately represent all the cognitive and affective variables that are integral to the concept of personality disorder" (621). Moreover, those personality disorders that have strong cognitive components are unlikely to fit on a circle, and so we need to ask ourselves this question: What other structure might represent them? We have already seen in the last chapter, in connection with the ordering of verbal and numerical abilities (Bynner & Romney 1986), that cognitive abilities are more likely to reveal themselves in a linear ordering or *simplex*. Consequently, we set out to determine whether the relationships between five personality disorders that could not be represented by a circular structure in our previous analyses could in fact conform to the pattern of a simplex.

The correlations among antisocial, borderline, avoidant, passive-aggressive, and compulsive personality disorders ascertained by Kass and colleagues (1985) and by Hyler and Lyons (1988) provided the data for this study. Schizotypal personality disorder was discarded, because we felt that it overlapped unduly with schizoid personality disorder.

Close inspection of the two correlation matrices revealed that the correlations did approximately conform to the simplex pattern. In a perfect simplex, the correlation matrices within a diagonal are equal to each other, and the coefficients decline progressively in magnitude as they move further away from the main diagonal (see Table 3.7). It would be extremely rare, however, for any correlation matrix on sample data to possess *all* the features of a simplex matrix and the most we can expect is an approximation. To test just how well the data did fit the simplex model, the correlation matrices were analyzed using the LISREL VI computer program (Jöreskog & Sörbom 1984). In this analysis, we employed the generalized least-squares method for estimating parameters in order to be consistent with our previous study (Romney & Bynner 1989). As with the circumplex, the simplex was tested under two separate conditions: (1) a model in which it is assumed that the disorders are assessed perfectly reliably, and (2) a quasi-simplex model, in which the correlations are corrected for attenuation (measurement error).

The data from Kass and colleagues (1985) fit the simplex model very well under the first condition. To achieve such a good fit, however, we had to do some fine tuning, correcting one of the variables (avoidant personality disorder) for attenuation. Although the Hyler and Lyons (1988) data did not fit the simplex model quite so well, even after correction of the same variable for attenuation, this particular ordering of the variables resulted in a better fit than any other ordering. It should be noted that the quasi-simplex model, in which *every* variable is corrected for attenuation, resulted in an uninterpretable output with parameter estimates assuming impossible values. Hence this model was rejected as inappropriate. An alternative to the simplex model is the single-factor model, but it failed to fit the data as well as the simplex model. See Table 3.8 for the respective goodness-of-fit values.

The simplex model with the better fit was obtained from the data derived from the larger sample and consequently inspires more confidence

Table 3.7
Representation of a Simplex-Correlation Matrix

	1	2	3	4	5
1	1				
2	r_1	1			
3	r_2	r_1	1		
4	r_3	r_2	r_1	1	
5	r_4	r_3	r_2	r_1	1

Table 3.8
Goodness-of-Fit Values for Simplex and Factor Models

1985 data

Model	χ^2	df	AGFI	RMS
Simplex	11.54	5	.974	.036
Factor	37.90	5	.963	.077

1988 data

Simplex	29.23	5	.921	.074
Factor	43.51	5	.927	.101

---

in its validity. Only one of the personality disorders in this simplex model, avoidant personality disorder, had to be corrected for attenuation, implying that the others could be measured more reliably. It should be noted that in this respect the simplex model differs from the circumplex model where *all* the personality disorder measures had to be corrected for attenuation in order to obtain a good fit with the data.

The simplex model shows how five personality disorders fall on a unidimensional scale running from antisocial at one end through borderline, avoidant, and passive-aggressive to compulsive at the other end. If we focus on the personality disorders at opposite ends of the continuum (i.e., antisocial and compulsive personality disorders), the dimension being measured seems to be similar to the novelty-seeking dimension proposed by Cloninger (1987) in his theoretical classification of personality variants. He states: "Individuals who are higher than average in novelty seeking . . . are characterized as impulsive, exploratory, fickle, excitable, quick-tempered, extravagant, and disorderly. . . . They are said to neglect details and are quickly distracted or bored. . . . In contrast, individuals who are lower than average in novelty seeking . . . often become preoccupied with narrowly defined focused details and require considerable thought before making decisions" (575).

The simplex is essentially a fixed sequence of variables or a stochastic process in which the probability of one variable's occurrence depends on the probability of occurrence of the variable preceding it in the chain. The inference to be drawn from this particular simplex is that there is a progressive change in novelty-seeking behavior as we move from one personality disorder to another, starting with antisocial personality disorder and finishing with compulsive personality disorder. Knowing what we do of these personality disorders, this inference is congruent with clinical expectations. It is well known that people with antisocial personalities are easily bored and seek thrills and other distractions, whereas people with compulsive disorders are just the opposite—they insist on sameness and cannot bear to have their routine disturbed. People with borderline, avoidant, and passive-aggressive personality disorders should be intermediate with respect to this characteristic.

THE CIRCUMPLEX, THE SIMPLEX, AND THE BIG FIVE

The complex dimension being represented by the simplex may also be viewed as a fusion of neuroticism and (lack of) conscientiousness, which are two of the Big Five dimensions of personality (Norman 1963; Wiggins & Trapnell, in press). Wiggins and Pincus (1989), using EFA, found that the five personality disorders on the simplex loaded significantly on neuroticism and conscientiousness. We would argue from our own research, however, that the two factors cannot be separated and that Wiggins and Pincus' conclusion that two common factors underlie these five personality disorders is mistaken in view of our discovery of a simplex pattern that accounts for the intercorrelations. Interestingly enough, their other findings showed that the remaining personality disorders, except for schizotypal personality disorder, loaded significantly on two of the other three Big Five factors, extroversion and agreeableness. These latter two dimensions correspond to the two principal axes of the circumplex, extroversion corresponding to power or dominance and agreeableness to affiliation. But the data of Wiggins and Pincus (1989) suggest that avoidant and antisocial personality disorders should fit onto both the circumplex and the simplex. These results, which were derived from *normal* subjects, are at variance with our own, and they deserve further investigation. Meanwhile, although we would not challenge the fact that individuals with avoidant and antisocial personality disorders have problems in interacting with others, we would argue that these problems are secondary rather than primary in nature.

The final factor of the Big Five, openness to experience, seems to be reserved for the schizotypal personality disorder alone. We did not include this disorder in any of our analyses because of its confusion with schizoid personality disorder. In any case, the high specificity of this factor makes it unlikely to fit on either the circumplex or the simplex. Deciding to ignore schizotypal personality disorder turned out to be a serendipitous act on our part.

IMPLICATIONS FOR PSYCHIATRIC CLASSIFICATION

The main implication of our findings for diagnosis is that there are essentially two types of personality disorders, those in which the primary deficit is interpersonal (the circumplex group) and those in which the primary deficit is cognitive (the simplex group). This implication is at odds with the current position taken by psychiatrists that the personality disorders can be subclassified into the three types (A, B, and C). As we have already mentioned, the arrangement of the interpersonal disorders around the circle is compatible with this clustering insofar as those disorders in the same cluster are close to each other on the circle, and disorders in the same cluster are juxtaposed on the simplex; that is, antisocial and borderline fall in cluster B (emotional), and avoidant, passive-aggressive, and compulsive fall in cluster C (fearful). We would nevertheless argue in favor of our own dichotomous subclassification of the personality disorders in terms of cognitive and interpersonal disorders on the grounds that not only does it fit the data well according to SEM goodness-of-fit indices, but it is theoretically more sound and of greater utility. The distinction between personality disorders that are primarily interpersonal and those that are primarily cognitive is consonant with both clinical intuition and empirical evidence.

NEW STRATEGIES FOR TREATMENT

The circumplex model can assist us not only in describing accurately the interpersonal behavior of personality-disordered individuals but also in predicting the behavior of those who interact with the personality-disordered individual. This is because some interpersonal behaviors tend to elicit *reciprocal* responses from others (e.g., submission tends to draw out dominance—Kiesler 1983).

In those personality disorders not on the circle but on the straight line, the primary cognitive deficit, which involves novelty seeking, can and usually does lead to serious disruptions in interpersonal behavior. Individuals diagnosed with antisocial personality disorder are bound to have personality conflicts with other people, especially with those in authority. Similarly, compulsive individuals, at the other end of the scale, are so set in their ways and unable to compromise that they have problems in relating to other people.

We would argue on the basis of our findings that the interpersonal difficulties associated with the personality disorders on the simplex are *secondary* to the cognitive deficit. Behaviors exhibited by these personality-disordered individuals may elicit *corresponding* responses. Thus avoidant behavior on the part of an individual will encourage a corresponding avoidant reaction on the part of someone else, and antisocial behavior will tend to provoke antisocial behavior from others.

The recommended treatment for people with interpersonal personality disorders is *interpersonal therapy* (e.g., Horowitz & Vitkus 1986), which can be traced back to the interpersonal theory of Sullivan (1953). The details of interpersonal therapy are beyond our scope here, but in essence the interpersonal therapist uses the interpersonal circle to determine which reactions to client problems are therapeutic and which are not. For instance, dependent clients will tend to elicit from others reciprocal reactions, such as telling them what to do and thereby furthering their dependency. The therapist should, therefore, guard against such nontherapeutic reactions and instead encourage dependent clients to take responsibility for their own behavior and to become independent. This illustration is, of course, a simplification of what actually takes place in therapy, but it conveys the gist of what happens.

With respect to the personality disorders located on the simplex, we would ask that a different approach to therapy be considered. The simplex portrays a bipolar continuum with the desire for sameness (routine) on one side (compulsive and passive-aggressive personality disorders) and the desire for change (excitement) on the other side (antisocial and borderline personality disorders). In the middle is avoidant personality disorder, exemplified by the individual who would like to make new friends and experience novel situations but who is fearful of being embarrassed by the outcome. For these disorders we recommend that treatment be directed to normalizing the desires, so that antisocial individuals develop a tolerance for monotony and routine and compulsive individuals learn to think and do things in nonhabitual ways. Cognitive therapy or cognitive-behavioral therapy seems to be the treatment of choice for such disorders. Changing the faulty cognitions that underlie maladaptive behavior should cause the behavior itself to change. The application of cognitive therapy to the treatment of personality disorders is expanding rapidly (cf. Freeman, Pretzer, Fleming, & Simon 1990). There is now even a danger that cognitive therapy will be used indiscriminately in the treatment of personality disorders and not be limited to those personality disorders that should most benefit from it; namely, those that lie on the simplex. Treating interpersonal disorders with cognitive therapy may prove to be as inefficient as treating primarily cognitive disorders with interpersonal therapy.

ARE WE DELUDING OURSELVES?

We have until now been discussing hypothetical models and, to a lesser extent, their implications for practice. But do these models really work, or are we deluding ourselves? The proof of the pudding is definitely in the eating. Let us turn, therefore, to another example taken from the psychiatric literature.

The onset of paranoia is usually regarded as a gradual, insidious process resulting from continual rejection and failure. Psychodynamic theory states that, in response to our misfortunes, we may become angry, either turning our anger inwards (introjection) and blaming ourselves, which would precipitate a loss of self-esteem and feelings of depression, or else turning our anger outwards (projection) and coming to resent and blame others (Candido & Romney 1990). The latter option can start the predisposed individual (i.e., someone with a paranoid personality) on the downward path to paranoia and eventually to paranoid schizophrenia as the disorder progresses. In other words, according to this theory, the paranoid process develops in a linear fashion, passing from one stage to the next as pathology increases. Similarly, as patients recover, they are expected to follow the same route in reverse. The theory therefore embraces the familiar simplex model.

To test how well the simplex model of the paranoid process fitted the data, Romney (1987) used LISREL to reanalyze a correlation matrix of six paranoid features provided by Lorr (1964). In order of increasing severity, the paranoid features were the following: *hostile attitude, verbalized hostility, resentment, blaming others, delusions of persecution,* and *delusions of influence.* When the symptoms were arranged in this order and the simplex model (Figure 3.6) was tested against the data, the model fit almost perfectly: $\chi^2(6) = 2.4$, $p = .88$; AGFI = .991; RMS = .013. When the variables were reordered to ascertain whether other orderings would fit the data even better, the residuals assumed negative values, a theoretical impossibility indicating that the corresponding models were obviously false. An attempt was also made to fit a more parsimonious common-factor model to the data. This model turned out to be a poor fit ($\chi^2(9) = 53.74$, $p < .001$; AGFI = .865; RMS = .065), demonstrating that general factor models are not appropriate for simplical data.

Inspection of the path coefficients between the various sequential stages shows that the strongest link in the chain is between feeling resentment and blaming others ($\beta = .93$). Cognitive therapists who catch such patients at stage 3 and try to prevent them from progressing to stage 4 will probably be unsuccessful. The weakest link in the chain is between stages 5 and 6 ($\beta = .59$), and the second weakest link between stages 4 and 5 ($\beta = .64$).

Interestingly enough, these findings run counter to the traditional view held by psychiatrists that delusions are held with such conviction that they are unshakable and that any attempt on the part of the therapist to dislodge them is bound to meet with failure. How then do we reconcile this traditional view with the empirical evidence presented by the simplex

Figure 3.6
A Simplex Model of the Paranoid Process

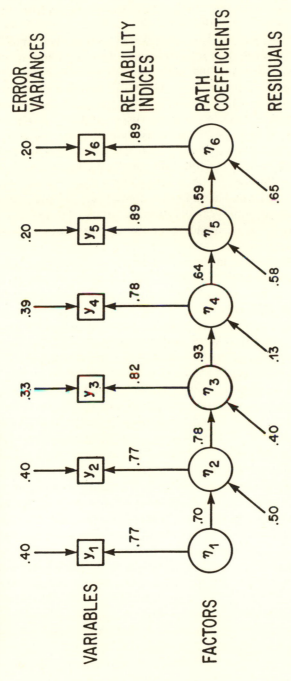

Key: 1. Hostile Attitude 2. Verbalized Hostility 3. Resentment 4. Blames Others 5. Delusions of Persecution 6. Delusions of Influence

Source: From "A Simplex Model of the Paranoid Process" by D. M. Romney, 1987, *Acta Psychiatrica Scandinavica, 75*, p. 653. Copyright 1987 by Munksgaard Publishers, Ltd. Reprinted by permission.

model? The traditional view has been attacked by Rudden, Gilmore, and Frances (1982), who relate anecdotal evidence of success in confronting paranoid subjects with their delusions during therapy, and more recently in an experimental study by Lowe and Chadwick (1990), who performed an experimental study on two separate cases. The first client in the experimental study was a twenty-nine-year-old British male, single and unemployed, who had a psychiatric history extending over five years. He presented with three distinct delusional beliefs, which he stated he had held for two years (belief 2) and four years (beliefs 1 and 3). His first belief was that he was engaged to be married to a woman called Amanda, with whom he had not been in contact for many years, and that she was reading his mind and controlling many of the things that were happening to him. His second belief was that he had been Jesus Christ in a previous life, and his third belief was that he had been Leonardo da Vinci in a previous life. The other client was a fifty-one-year-old married woman with no children. Her psychiatric history extended back over twenty years. She also held three separate beliefs, all for ten years. The first was that she was not yet twenty years old; the second was that she was the daughter of Princess Anne; and the third was that she had been raped on numerous occasions and had given birth to several children, each of whom had been taken away from her immediately.

In this study the clients were not told that their beliefs were a sign of illness but rather that they were reactions to particular experiences they had encountered. Moreover, they were not told outright that their delusional beliefs were wrong, but were asked to "suspend their conviction that their beliefs were undeniably true and to consider alternatives" (465). After discussing all the evidence in favor of the beliefs, the therapist first pointed out inconsistencies and irrationalities in the client's belief systems, and then went on to present an alternative explanation for what had been happening. The evidence strongly supporting this alternative explanation was made available by the therapist.

The degree of conviction with which the delusions were held was assessed before, during, and after treatment and at follow-up one month, three months, and six months later. After treatment, all three delusions in both clients were rejected totally, and they remained so at follow-up. By persistently challenging these clients' delusions, the therapists were able to eradicate them. This therapeutic success could have been predicted from the simplex diagram that shows that the chain was relatively weak at the more pathological end. Here then we have a fine illustration of how the modeling of the development of paranoia by means SEM helped us to decide what action to take to achieve a desired therapeutic outcome.

Chapter 4

Attitudes and the Self-Concept

Personality theorist Gordon Allport, reviewing the history of the attitude concept, described it as the "primary building stone in the edifice of social psychology" (Allport 1935). Fundamental to the way we relate to the social world and to ourselves as active agents within it are the attitudes we express. The essential elements of attitudes are cognitive, affective, and behavioral. "An attitude is an idea charged with emotion which predisposes a particular class of actions to a particular class of social situations" (Triandis 1971). Or more simply: "Attitudes concern feelings about particular social objects—physical objects, types of people, particular persons, social institutions, government policies, etc." (Nunnally 1978, 590).

So when we say that someone holds an attitude to something we imply that they have both some belief and some positive or negative feeling about it. We also imply that they have a predisposition to act in a certain way towards it. For example, an attitude to smoking involves a cognitive appraisal expressed in a belief (Smoking causes lung cancer—smoking does not cause lung cancer), an affective or emotional response to smoking (Smoking is bad—smoking is good), and a corresponding behavioral intention (If offered a cigarette I will not smoke it—if offered a cigarette I will smoke it).

In this chapter we shall be examining a particular attitude domain—the domain of personal or self-attitudes—or people's own feelings or attitudes toward themselves. The basic reasoning and methodology for research in this domain is derived from the wider range of research in social attitudes; in the interest of generality, therefore, we shall draw upon this as well.

ATTITUDE HIERARCHIES

The typical psychological conceptualization of attitudes sees them, like other personal characteristics, as organized hierarchically. Figure 4.1, taken from Eysenck (1957b), shows specific opinions or evaluative beliefs about particular topics at the bottom of the hierarchy. These are consid-

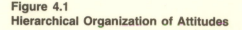

Figure 4.1
Hierarchical Organization of Attitudes

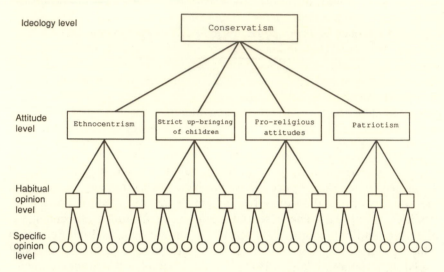

Source: From *The Psychology of Politics* (p. 112) by H. J. Eysenck, 1957, London: Routledge & Kegan Paul. Copyright 1957 by Routledge & Kegan Paul. Reprinted by
permission.

ered unstable and most easily subject to persuasion. At higher levels more
consistent predispositions, where opinions cohere into a particular attitude, are to be found. At a higher level still are values embracing interre-
lated sets of attitudes or ideologies. Thus in the field of politics, opinions
expressed about particular political events and policy issues—defense,
taxation, the environment—can be conceptualized as arising from more
deeply held predispositions or attitudes towards these subjects: For example, "defense is generally a good thing, so we should spend more
money on it," "reequip the armed forces," and so on. Similarly, "government spending is bad, so we should privatize public services," "cut
taxes," and so on. Lying behind such attitudes is the more general orientation identified with whole sets of attitudes: "right" (conservative) versus "left" (socialist or liberal or radical) ideology. Conservatism-liber-
alism (Eysenck 1957b) and authoritarianism-permissiveness (Adorno et
al. 1950) describe dimensions that operate at this most general level,
representing the interface between the evaluation of the social and personal world through attitudes and the deeper and more permanent features of personality or identity.

IDENTITY

As we have noted, attitudes can be expressed about a huge variety of social issues and personal matters, from capital punishment to whether or not premarital sex is acceptable. In total, attitudes represent one facet of identity; they are "that unique syndrome of psychological characteristics which differentiates one person from another" (Breakwell 1986, 10). Attitudes are the social component, representing the way in which people present themselves to others, the sort of person they would like other people to take them to be (Banks et al. 1991). Paralleling the way we present ourselves to others is the way we perceive and feel about ourselves. The self-concept is the sum total of attitudes people adopt toward themselves, their beliefs in themselves, their feelings about themselves, and their predispositions to change. Fueling the motivation to change personal identity is a process of self-evaluation that results in one's sense of self-esteem. Are they happy overall with their self-concepts, or do they wish to improve them? Traumatic experiences like failing an examination or losing a job threaten confidence and are said to damage self-esteem. To restore it they are impelled to act, either reappraising the value of the goal they have failed to achieve, or seeking other forms of achievement (e.g., success in sport or social life) as a compensation for the academic failure. This makes the point that people operate in many spheres of life, feeling satisfied with their performance in one domain, such as social life, while being dissatisfied with themselves in others, such as the school or the workplace (Harter 1985). Overall self-esteem is maintained by reconciling appraisals in one domain with those in the others. If self-esteem remains persistently low in all of them, then an individual may face serious psychological stress with depression, and even suicide as the ultimate outcome.

An important element of such evaluations is the extent to which people have confidence in their ability to function effectively in the different life domains. Self-efficacy combines feelings of competence with feelings of control (Bandura 1982). Political self-efficacy, for example, describes the extent to which people feel able to influence events politically as opposed to feeling politically impotent; occupational self-efficacy indicates the extent to which they feel able to perform their occupation competently.

Whatever basis identity has, whether identity is a biological characteristic present at birth (Eysenck 1970) or as a social construction reflecting the process of relating to others (Gergen 1971, 1987; Harré 1979), a sense of self-efficacy arises mainly through a learning process (Bandura 1982).

In this sense, self-efficacy both reflects the appraisals of others—teachers, employers, friends, and family—and spurs action to bring about improvement. The individual is both a product of social structure (which sets the goals and standards to aspire to) and an active agent making choices and directing behavior to bring about desirable ends (Markova 1987); that is, "a productive processor of reality" (Hurrelmann 1988).

A critical period in the formation of adult identity is adolescence, when certain crucial developmental tasks have to be performed (Erikson 1968). The individual has to learn to cope with physical and sexual maturation, gender roles, independence, occupational identity, and adult social relations (Hendry 1989). At different stages, the focus shifts: the resolution of an identity dilemma in social relations leads to a dilemma with sexuality, which in turn gives way to a dilemma with personal autonomy and relations with parents (Coleman 1974). At any point in time, therefore, the individual has a particular identity structure and is participating in a process bringing about change (Markova 1987).

The identity structure is where we may expect to find links between such characteristics as self-efficacy and other deeper and more lasting personality characteristics that perhaps have a biological base. The personality factor neuroticism (Eysenck 1957a), for example, has much in common with low self-efficacy because of the shared elements of negative self-appraisal. Other well-established facets of self-appraisal connect in various ways with the factor psychological estrangement, which represents psychologists' attempt to operationalize the sociological concept of alienation (Hammond 1988). This concept implies a degree of self-derogation and also has many features in common with low self-efficacy and neuroticism. Locus of control or attribution style (Rotter 1966), which expresses the extent to which people believe that events are controlled by themselves or external forces, also has an element of self-deprecation in it. Those who believe in an external locus of control are in effect conceding their own lack of self-efficacy. The distinctive feature of all these personal perceptions of the self is that they have both positive and negative connotations. In this sense they may all be appropriately described as attitudes.

It is not surprising that those who focus on the structural as opposed to the process features of the self-concept seek to show that all of these supposedly separate components of self-appraisal may be seen as different aspects of some underlying personality trait or traits. The evidence as before is provided by correlation. A moderately high degree of positive intercorrelation among all self-attitudes is seen as pointing to a single factor underlying them. The alternative process conception maintains the separateness of the self-attitudes using their intercorrelation to help unravel the dynamics of the interactions among them. Critical to both conceptions are the measurements involved. This takes us to the question of how to measure attitudes.

ATTITUDE MEASUREMENT

Factor theory implies that attitudes and opinions arise from, rather than influence, more deeply held predispositions. The influence is seen as predominantly one-way. The factor-theory approach to measurement similarly directs attention to opinions as indicators of more deeply held beliefs. Consequently, the assessment of an attitude typically involves aggregating responses across sets of opinion items considered to measure or "index" the attitude (Dawes 1972).

In relation to self-attitudes, there are three principal ways in which such assessment is achieved. The first is through a battery of opinion items aggregated to produce a composite measure of the attitude they have in common using what is known as "Likert scaling." The second entails ratings of the self-concept on a battery of personal characteristics in the form of bipolar scales in what is known as the "semantic differential" format (Osgood, Suci, & Tannenbaum 1957). The third involves the use of standardized inventories combining elements of the previous two and designed to measure particular features of the self-concept. Rosenberg's Self-Esteem Scale (1965), for example, is composed of six items, each of which requires a response of endorsement or rejection. The basic principles of measurement are most easily described through the Likert approach.

In "Likert scaling" (Likert 1932), respondents are invited to express agreement or disagreement with statements about social issues or personal characteristics on a five-point (or longer) scale ranging from "strongly agree" through "agree," "can't decide," "disagree," and "strongly disagree." Thus respondents may be asked to indicate their agreement or disagreement with such statements as these: "I usually find it very difficult to get on at social gatherings," or "I find it easy to learn new skills." The response to each item is assigned a score from 1 to 5, and the total score expressing the overall attitude is obtained by adding together the scores on the individual items.

Critical in developing a set of opinion items to form an attitude scale is to establish that the items are positively correlated. In the extreme case, unrelated items or items that are negatively related to the others will produce a score that is uninterpretable. Technically, summation of scores from correlated items accumulates common variance or communality among them and increases reliability of the composite as random-error variance cancels out. The usual first step in the modern use of such attitude scaling, therefore, is to test the dimensionality of the set of items to determine whether the items can be considered to form a single dimension and can be sensibly combined to form the scale. The solution to the problem, as will be obvious now from previous chapters, is a factor-

analytic one (Oppenheim 1966; McKennell 1970). Given an attitude domain and a set of opinion items generated from raw expressions of opinion
about it, what then is the minimum number of dimensions that we need to
represent the items and which items fall closest to, and hence can be used
to measure, each dimension? Factor analysis is typically used to find the
answers, generating one or more attitude dimensions that can be measured and used to summarize the whole domain. In this sense, factor
analysis plays the role both of uncovering dimensions and of testing hypotheses about the dimensionality of the attitude domain. Factor analysis
helps to validate the measurement hypotheses that certain items are expressions of deeper attitude constructs; as a result factor loadings are
often described (wrongly in our view) as "validity coefficients" (Heise &
Bohrnstedt 1970).

In accordance with the hierarchical model that lies behind such a validation procedure, the correlations between the attitudes can themselves
be factor analyzed, producing a smaller number of more fundamental
dimensions. In an exactly comparable way to the measurement of intelligence, all opinions and attitudes can be reduced ultimately to one or two
basic factors.

Osgood's semantic-differential technique introduces further complexities in technique but still conforms to the same basic factor model. A set
of social objects, such as "smoker," "mother," "myself," are rated by
respondents on a set of bipolar scales such as "hot–cold," "good–bad."
In between are various gradations of the attribute with a "neutral" category in the middle: The number of scale points varies between three and
seven. In the original use of the method, large numbers of concepts were
assessed on large numbers of scales; then, by averaging the rating scores
across the concepts and by factor analyzing their intercorrelations, three
broad dimensions of "connotative" meaning were identified: evaluation,
potency, and activity. The evaluation factor, of course, reflects attitude
towards the concept: "I like myself—I don't like myself." In later uses of
the technique, more restricted content domains have been examined using
relatively small numbers of concepts and a limited number of scales designed specifically to assess the characteristics of the concepts, that is,
beliefs about the concepts. In the version known as the "personality
differential" (Hallworth 1965), the self-concept, ideal self-concept, or the
concept of any other person is rated on a set of personality descriptions
such as "sociable—unsociable." In line with the original analysis strategy, "personality factors" can be extracted from the cross-concept correlations, or else the correlations between scales can be analyzed for each
concept separately.

The assumptions implicit in attitude-scaling approaches will be clear
from previous chapters. Again the existence of correlation is used to
justify a hierarchical model of human characteristics; and alternative con-

ceptualizations are typically disregarded. But an important distinction needs to be made. The measurement of opinions, the raw material of attitudes, is notoriously unreliable. Placing a lot of weight on a single expression of opinion about personal competence (such as "I do not give up easily") is inadvisable because of the volatility of such opinions, as reflected in their generally weak correlations with other variables. It is therefore sensible to aggregate scores from correlated opinion items to produce a composite-attitude variable with greater reliability. But the factor-analysis model advances claims that the correlations among items is evidence of the composite variable's validity. Correlation is a necessary condition, of course, for validating factorially produced composites at different levels of a hierarchy, but it is clearly not a sufficient condition because many other forms of the model conform to the correlations equally well (Bynner 1987, 1990; Pawson 1980).

The significance of the argument is more striking in the study of attitudes than perhaps in any other area of personal characteristics, as will become clearer through the examples examined in this chapter; we shall further elaborate this argument in the final chapter of the book. In line with the traditional conceptualization, it is commonplace for psychologists to think of opinions and attitudes as residing in relatively fixed ideological or personality structures that may be influenced marginally but rarely changed fundamentally. Yet education, not to mention advertising and political propaganda, is premised on almost the opposite assumption, namely that given the right circumstances and the right approaches, attitudes can be changed (Bandura 1982; Triandis 1971). The process conception of dynamic attitude structures, which shows affective and behavioral elements interacting and being modified in response to new information and experience, lies at the heart of personal agency, and is reflected much better by dynamic structural models than by static factor models. Such structural models also offer the prospect of better insight into how attitudes may be changed. In what follows, we demonstrate applications of this approach through a number of examples from self-attitude research.

STRUCTURE OF THE SELF-CONCEPT

We shall start with an analysis from studies of teenage smoking in which the original goal was to fit a hierarchical model to self-image data by means of the semantic-differential technique.

The example here is taken from a research project in England and Wales (Bynner 1969, 1981), in which 5,601 boys aged eleven to fifteen rated four concepts—the self, the ideal self, the teenage smoker, and the teenage nonsmoker—on a set of thirteen scales (see Table 4.1).

We shall look at two outcomes of the analysis: (1) the development and

Table 4.1
Factor Loadings for First-Order Factors

Scales	f1	f2	f3	f4	f5	Residual variance
1. Gentle – Tough	60	0	0	0	0	64
2. Good fighter – Not much of a fighter	-64	0	0	0	0	59
3. A bit of a sissy – Tough	58	0	0	0	0	66
4. Interested in girls – Not interested in girls	0	0	0	0	0	37
5. Try to attract girls Do not try to attract girls	0	-79	0	0	0	38
6. Like to be alone – Like to be with a group	0	0	57	0	0	68
7. Have many friends – Have one or two friends	0	0	-49	0	0	76
8. Good at school work Not so good at school work	0	0	0	-49	0	76
9. Often successful – Often a failure	0	0	0	-52	0	73
10. Plan and think ahead – Cannot wait; want every- thing at once	0	0	0	-37	0	87
11. Often disobedient – Usually do as told	0	0	0	0	59	65
12. Like to do forbidden things – Do not do forbidden things	0	0	0	0	56	69
13. Spend my money – Save my money	0	0	0	0	34	85

Note: Decimal points are omitted for all factor loadings and residual variances.

testing of a measurement (factor) model for the self-image data and (2) the testing of a higher-order factor model designed to show relations between the constructs of the measurement model and then to allow the reconstruction of the factor model as a structural model. The aim in developing the measurement model for the self-image data was to identify the minimum number of dimensions in terms of which it could be described; each of these corresponds to a self-image component. Initial analysis (Bynner & Coxhead 1979; Coxhead & Bynner 1981) had suggested that the most appropriate model for describing the four concepts contained five first-order factors labeled "toughness," "precocity," "sociability," "successfulness," and "conformity," which could themselves be reduced to two higher-order factors, "school values" (successfulness and conformity) and "teenage values" (toughness, precocity, and sociability). This model conforms with the arguments of such writers as Sugarman (1967), who saw adolescent values as displaying two major orientations, one toward or against the world of school and adults (where conventional educational achievements are valued) and the other toward or against the values of teenage culture (social achievements, especially success with the opposite sex) operating largely outside the school. In other words, the first-order factors may be seen as displaying relatively specific characteristics of the four concepts and the second-order factors display more general characteristics concerned with, on the one hand, the values of the school, and, on the other, the values of the peer group. In relation to the self-image data, the model provides personal appraisals at two levels, broadly linked with social life and school achievement.

MEASUREMENT MODEL FOR THE SELF-IMAGE DATA

Table 4.2 shows the result, using LISREL, of fitting the first-order five-factor model to the self-image data and comparing it with more restrictive models comprising two, three, and four factors. Table 4.1 gives the estimated factor loadings for the five-factor model. Note that all values of factor loadings, other than those for which estimates are given, were constrained to be zero. Two criteria are used for assessing the fit of the model: χ^2 divided by df (Wheaton et al. 1977) and the maximum residual correlation (max r), which is independent of sample size. A reasonable fit *for a sample of this size* corresponds to a χ^2 ratio of eleven and a maximum residual correlation of .10. The figures in Table 4.2 point clearly to the superiority of the five-factor model over the other models. As we move from two to five factors, there is a large drop in the χ^2 ratio and an equally striking fall in the size of the maximum residual correlation. For two factors, the highest correlation left after fitting the model in the smoking study is .32. For five factors in the smoking study, it drops to .09. The analysis confirms the findings of the exploratory analysis that five factors are optimal for describing the self-image.

Table 4.2
Goodness-of-Fit Indices for Different Models for the Smoking Study Self-Image Data

No. of Factors	χ^2	df	χ^2/df	Max r	Ave r
2 Factors	3326	53	62.75	0.32	–
3 Factors	1529	51	29.98	0.27	–
4 Factors	1129	58	19.40	0.24	–
5 Factors	1125	55	10.87	0.09	–
Higher Order Factor Model	739	63	11.79	.13	.031
First Causal Model	644	63	10.72	.12	.026
Second Causal Model	644	69	9.33	.12	.025

RECONSTRUCTION OF THE MODEL
FOR THE SELF-IMAGE DATA

The five factors can be identified with five separate self-image components, an interpretation that raises the question of how these components are related among themselves. The correlations among the factors point to two broad clusters corresponding to the two higher-order factors postulated earlier in line with Sugarman's theory. The fitted-hierarchical model for these relationships is shown in Figure 4.2, in which the five factors are reduced to two more general orientations, identified with teenage values and school values respectively. Although the χ^2 ratio was a respectable 11.79 and the maximum residual correlation was .13, the model was clearly faulty as shown by the factor loading and residual variance for factor 2 on factor 5. Both massively exceed one, and the latter is negative. These are meaningless results for a factor model in which all factor loadings must be less than one and all residual variances must be positive. Consequently we conclude that our postulated two major orientations in adolescent self-perception, as supported by exploratory factor analysis, are false. Further examination of the correlations, coupled with insights gained from delinquency theory (e.g., Matza 1964), suggested an alternative structural model for the constructs. In this model (Figure 4.3), we postulated one construct identified with a nonconforming or delinquent

Figure 4.2
Parameter Estimates for Higher-Order Factor Model

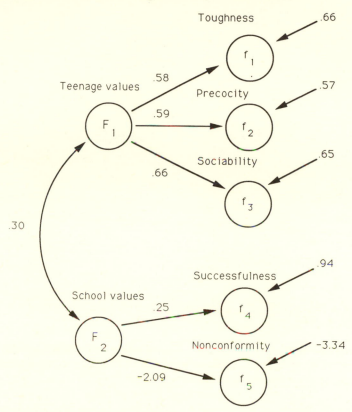

f_1	1.00				
f_2	.35	1.00			
f_3	.39	.39	1.00		
f_4	-.04	-.04	-.05	1.00	
f_5	.37	.37	.41	-.51	1.00

Correlations between factors

Source: From "Theory, Data and Observational Relations: A Structural Modelling Approach" by J. M. Bynner, 1988, *International Review of Sociology, 3,* p. 239. Copyright by Franco Angeli. Reprinted by permission.

Figure 4.3
Causal Model for Relations Between Self-Image Constructs

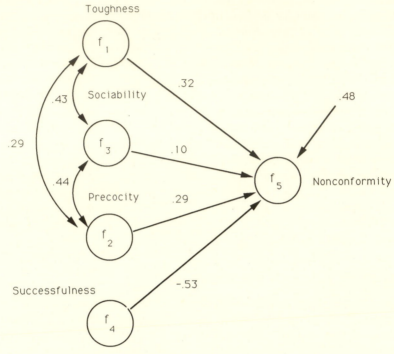

Source: From "Theory, Data and Observational Relations: A Structural Modelling Approach"
by J. M. Bynner, 1988, *International Review of Sociology, 3,* p. 241. Copyright 1988
by Franco Angeli. Reprinted by permission.

orientation as arising from or being characterized by, on the one hand, toughness, precocity, and sociability and, on the other hand, by educational failure. This model has a slightly improved fit (χ^2 ratio 10.72 and maximum residual correlation now .12), and all the parameter estimates are readily interpretable.

The relationships in this model pointed to further ways of improving it, which again seemed theoretically sensible. Toughness and precocity are again in a sense appraisals of current behavior and attitudes—mixing with the opposite sex and exhibiting the values of teenage masculinity (toughness and the ability to fight). Sociability, on the other hand, has more of the overtones of a temperamental trait, with links perhaps to the personality factor extroversion. Accordingly, a further variant of the model presenting these possibilities was formulated, with sociability preceding toughness and precocity in the causal sequence. This second causal model proved to have a better fit than the previous one, suggesting that a sequential ordering of the characteristics provided the most plausible interpretation of the data.

Substantively the results of this analysis suggest that nonconformity in young people is built up through the development of characteristics of two kinds. One kind of characteristic is associated with toughness and precocity, the central values of (male) youth culture, participation in which is contingent upon a degree of sociability. The other characteristic is rooted in experience in the education system, especially in whether the young person perceives himself as successful in it. Thus a combination of participation in and endorsement of the values of teenage culture, coupled with perceived poor performance at school, underpins nonconformity. This is the characteristic that, of all those studied, related most closely to self-reported teenage delinquency. Other analyses, not reported here, place the *ideal* self-image high on toughness and precocity and educational success. Clearly to reverse the trend towards a delinquent orientation, more needs to be done to bolster the self-images of those performing least well at school. This possibility is pursued in the next analysis, which uses data collected from U.S. teenagers.

SELF-CONCEPT AND DELINQUENCY

The United States Youth and Transition Study (Bachman, O'Malley, & Johnston 1978; Bynner, O'Malley, & Bachman 1981) measured the educational achievement, behavior attitudes, and background characteristics of a national sample of 1471 school boys. Data were collected at five time points, starting when the boys were in their tenth grade: 1966, 1968, 1969, 1970, and 1974. For the purposes of this analysis, data were used from the 1966 and 1968 sweep when the boys' ages were sixteen and eighteen respectively. The following variables were used in the analysis: (1) socioeconomic status or SES (defined as the mean of six family-background items, including father's occupation), (2) self-concept school ability (an index of three items reflecting respondent's rating of himself in comparison with others of his age on overall school ability), (3) self-esteem (a ten-item index adapted from the Rosenberg Scale; see Rosenberg 1965), (4) anomie (a self-assessment based on eight items derived from the Srole Scale; see Srole 1956), and (5) delinquent behavior in school (derived from the frequency of occurrence of seven different types of delinquent behavior in school.)

The self-appraisal measures in this list—self-concept school ability, self-esteem, anomie, and delinquent behavior in school—showed sufficient intercorrelation to try fitting a single-factor model to the data. Table 4.3 shows the results, including the goodness-of-fit indices at the two time points, 1966 and 1968.

The fit is poor at both time points. Also, one variable alone, self-

Table 4.3
Goodness-of-Fit Indices for Youth-in-Transition Self-Attitude Data

Model	χ^2	df	AGFI	RMS	Max r
Single Factor Model					
1966	58	2	.91	.05	.10
1968	34	2	.94	.04	.09
Anchored Simplex Model					
1966	4	2	.99	.01	—
1968	9	2	.98	.02	—

esteem, overwhelms the rest in the definition of the factor with by far the highest loading: .84 in sweep one and .998 in sweep two. A factor loading of .998 suggests that self-esteem is virtually identical with the factor. The model merely reinforces the picture that we have presented earlier of self-concept measures typically converging into a single assessment of affect. This provides little information that can be used to suggest how negative feelings can be reduced and how their ultimate outcome, delinquency, may be inhibited. Again we can seek an alternative in a structural model, this one referring to theories of delinquency such as those of Matza (1964), Cloward and Ohlin (1960), and Kaplan (1975), who see an important element of delinquency as residing in the negative appraisals of poor performance at school. To represent this possibility, we constructed a simplex model containing the four variables used in the factor model and a fifth variable, SES, which is used to "anchor" the simplex, as in the analysis of cognitive abilities reported in chapter 2. Figure 4.4 shows the results of fitting this model to the data at the two time points.

The fit of the model to the data is substantially improved, as shown by the χ^2 ratio and the maximum residual correlations (see Table 4.3). In line with theory, the results also make good substantive sense with low socioeconomic status underpinning the first of three attitude measures that form a sequence preceding delinquency. First, a poor self-concept in relation to school ability lies closest in the causal chain to social class; this is followed by reduced self-esteem, which itself appears to feed a growing sense of alienation or anomie and ultimately the increased likelihood of delinquency in school.

Figure 4.4
Causal Model for Youth-in-Transition Study

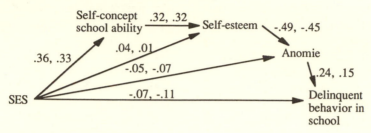

Note: The first value in each pair is for the 1966 data, and the second is for the 1968 data.

Some explanation of the use of SES to anchor the simplex is necessary. In the absence of the social class measure, there is no logical reason why the flow of influence should not run from delinquency through anomie through self-esteem to self-concept for school ability. When this possibility is reflected in a reformulated model with the directions reversed, the fit is substantially reduced. In this case we can see social class—a fixed antecedent condition in young people's backgrounds—as anchoring the linear sequence by showing which linear order is superior. Educational attainment moderates the effects of social class on the self-concept of school ability and on the characteristics that follow the latter in the causal chain. We thus have a model for the relation of school failure to delinquency that makes good empirical and theoretical sense.

SELF-EFFICACY AND ESTRANGEMENT

Data from a study of economic and political socialization in teenagers—the 16–19 Initiative (Bynner 1987; Banks et al. 1991)—enable us to extend our exploration of the self-concept. Two cohorts of young people (aged fifteen to sixteen and seventeen to eighteen, respectively) sampled from four U.K. areas completed questionnaires in 1987, 1988, and 1989. One of the questionnaires contained fourteen Likert-style opinion items on different facets of the self-concept, ranging from "I find it easy to make new friends" to "I give up easily." These items, together with others, had been used in previous research to operationalize two postulated dimensions of the self-concept, self-efficacy (Sherer, Maddux, & Mercandante 1982), and psychological estrangement (Hammond 1988). Exploratory factor analysis suggested that four factors provided the best fit to the data at the first level and could be labeled self-esteem (e.g., I am happy to be the person I am), depression (e.g., I sometimes wonder if anything is worthwhile), self-confidence (e.g., I seem to be capable of handling most problems in life), and motivation (e.g., If I can't do a job the first time I keep trying until I can). But at a second level of analysis these four factors reduced to two—the postulated self-efficacy (motivation and self-confidence) and estrangement (low self-esteem and depression).

The four first-order factors were quite highly intercorrelated, as were the two second-order factors (.80), suggesting that all the original fourteen items might be reduced ultimately to a single factor. This possibility could be set against the two-factor explanation. As Table 4.4 shows, the fit for the single general factor was poor. The two-factor model fitted the data much better, a finding which suggested that self-efficacy and estrangement provided the best explanation of the correlations among the items. However, an examination of the correlations between the four first-order factors pointed to other possibilities. There was a clear simplex pattern.

Table 4.4
Goodness-of-Fit Indices for 16–19 Initiative Self-Attitude Data

Model	χ^2	df	χ^2/df	AGFI	RMS
One-factor Model					
1987	101	2	50.5	.95	.03
1988	82	2	41.0	.95	.03
Two-factor Model					
1987	3	1	3.0	.99	.00
1988	5	1	5.0	.99	.01
Quasi-simplex Model a					
1987	3	1	3.0	.99	.00
1988	5	1	5.0	.99	.01
Quasi-simplex Model b					
1987	.2	1	.2	1.00	.002
1988	.4	1	.4	1.00	.002

Table 4.4 also shows the results of fitting a quasi-simplex (i.e., with measurement errors included) to the correlation data for the first-order factors (model a). The fit indices are identical to those for the two-factor solution. The path coefficients are shown in Figure 4.5.

The first interesting point about this analysis is that as far as goodness-of-fit is concerned, there is nothing to choose between the two-factor model and the quasi-simplex model. We are faced, therefore, with a choice between them that has to be based on other theoretical considerations. The two-factor model takes the self-concept measures back towards general appraisal within the personality; it gives few hints as to how any one of the four factors might change in response to changes in another. The simplex model, on the other hand, does precisely this. It suggests that lowered self-esteem leads to depression that itself reduces self-confidence. At the end of the chain, there is a reduction in motivation, the basis of achievement, in which self-esteem typically resides. The vicious circle implied describes a maladaptive learning process and points to the ways of inhibiting it. Changing the strength or even reversing the direction of any one of the four elements in the simplex for an individual teenager is likely to change all of them.

Finally we examined the effect on the model of introducing two other attitude variables: locus of economic control and political cynicism. The former was assessed by a nine-item Likert scale comprised of such items as "Getting a job today is just a matter of chance," and "People who are

Figure 4.5
16–19 Initiative: Self-Concept Data

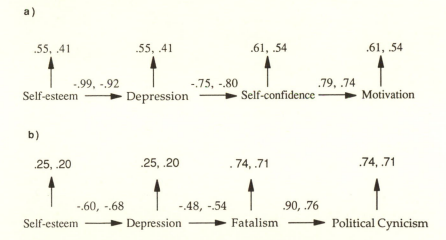

Note: The first value in each pair is for the 1987 data, and the second value is for the 1988 data.

successful in their work generally deserve it." Political cynicism (Marsh 1977) was measured by three items: "Politicians are in politics for their own benefit and not for the benefit of the community," "It does not really make much difference which political party is in power in Britain," and "None of the political parties would do anything to benefit me." We constructed a quasi-simplex in which self-esteem preceded depression, as in the previous analysis; this time, however, depression was followed by locus of control (fatalism) and then by political cynicism. Table 4.4 shows the goodness-of-fit indices for the quasi-simplex model (model b), and Figure 4.5 shows the parameter estimates.

Again the superiority of the quasi-simplex model is apparent. The nearly perfect fit reaffirms the power of the simplex to represent the relations between the self-attitudes. Self-esteem can be seen as dictating in individuals the levels not only of depression but of locus of control and ultimately of political cynicism as well. Thus individuals with low self-esteem become first depressed, then convinced that events in their lives are controlled by others. The consequence is a growing cynicism about political institutions and politics, which are symbols of the adult world where the loss of self-esteem originates.

QUALITY OF LIFE AND HEALTH CARE

Finally we turn to another situation where self-attitudes have an important part to play—quality of life. The quality of life of individuals suffering from chronic physical ailments is the subject of much discussion. Is it a unitary dimension? Or is it made up of several components? A study by Jenkins and Stanton (1984) applied "before and after surgery a comprehensive research protocol to assess changes in people who had undergone elective cardiac operations" (287).

Follow-up data were collected on 469 patients six months after the date of surgery, using over fifty items and scales that were then subjected to a series of factor analyses (Jenkins, Jono, Stanton, & Stroup 1990). Five factors emerged which were identified with "recovery dimensions": (1) morale ("giving up," hopelessness, helplessness), (2) symptoms of illness (chest pain or pressure or heaviness, shortness of breath, insomnia, and fatigue), (3) neurological dysfunction (e.g., memory loss), (4) interpersonal relationships (getting along with other people), and (5) socioeconomic status (decrease in income, job status, and capability). The highest correlations among the factors were between low morale and symptoms of illness and between low morale and poor interpersonal relationships, indicating the central importance of the morale factor. In fact, this factor was responsible for almost half of the variance accounted for by the five factors.

Because the factors were intercorrelated, the first task was to determine whether these intercorrelations could be explained by a higher-order factor representing quality of life as a single general dimension (Romney, Jenkins, & Bynner 1992). However, this single-factor model had a poor fit to the data (Table 4.5). Attention was therefore directed to alternative structural models containing pathways running between the five factors that might account for the data better and also be theoretically satisfying. In this particular example, however, the direction in which the pathways run becomes the critical issue.

It seems self-evident that chronic physical illness has a demoralizing effect on individuals and diminishes their sense of well-being. Feeling unwell and being incapacitated are bound after a while to "get one down," reduce the desire and opportunity for social interaction, and cause absenteeism or diminished efficiency at work. But there have also been countless studies showing that the reverse is true: Individuals who are under stress, who are worried and unhappy, and who are socially isolated are more prone to physical illness, suffer from physical illness more profoundly, take longer to recover, are more likely to relapse, and generally have a decreased life expectancy (see Berkman & Syme 1979). The first model is consistent with the conventional medical view, and the second model is consistent with the psychosomatic view. The first model suggests that deterioration in health causally precedes psychosocial and economic factors; that is, symptoms of illness and neurological dysfunction adversely affect interpersonal relationships, morale, and socioeconomic status. To this was added the postulate that the latter three factors would themselves follow a causal order, from socioeconomic status to morale to

Table 4.5
Goodness-of-Fit Indices for the Health-Related Quality-of-Life Data

Model	χ^2	df	χ^2/df	AGFI	RMS
Single-Factor Model	55.00	5	11.00	.851	.080
Medical Model a	1.82	1	1.18	.998	.012
Medical Model b	3.24	3	1.04	.995	.016
Psychosomatic Model a	40.40	5	8.08	.905	.065
Psychosomatic Model b	28.21	3	9.40	.886	.054

interpersonal relationships. The alternative (psychosomatic) model proposes that neurological dysfunction and diminished socioeconomic status result in reduced morale, which in turn aggravates symptoms of illness and disrupts interpersonal relationships. This causal ordering reflects the accepted belief that some illness symptoms are psychosomatic; that is, they arise from, or are exacerbated by, low morale, as distinct from being responsible for low morale. Both models were tested against the recovery study data to ascertain which model had the better fit; that is, which of the two models explains more of the variance and covariance in the correlation matrix of the factor scores.

Two versions of the medical model were tested. In the first model (medical model a), paths were drawn from symptoms of illness and neurological dysfunction to poor relationships, low morale, and diminished socioeconomic status (SES), respectively. Another path was drawn from diminished SES to low morale, and yet another from low morale to poor relationships. This was a model with a good fit: The χ^2 ratio dropped to 1.8, and the AGFI rose to .998 (Table 4.5). However, because the coefficient for the path from symptoms to relationships was a negligible .04 and because the coefficient from dysfunction to morale was a negligible .03, these two pathways were eliminated and the model was tested again. The goodness-of-fit indices for this model variant (medical model b) were barely changed. On the grounds of parsimony, therefore, this variant of model 1 represented a definite improvement on the previous one. The parameter estimates for the model are shown in Figure 4.6.

The alternative Figure 4.7 tested the second hypothesis. Paths were drawn from neurological dysfunction and diminished SES to low morale and from low morale to symptoms of illness and poor relationships. The goodness-of-fit indices for this model (psychosomatic model a) showed that the model did not fit the data well: The χ^2 ratio rose to 8 and the AGFI dropped to .905. However, because poor relationships can adversely affect morale (Greenblatt, Becerra, & Serafetinides 1982), as well as the other way round, the model was tested once again with a path leading from relationships to morale instead of from morale to relationships (psychosomatic model b). The goodness-of-fit indices for this model variant showed no improvement (Table 4.5). The psychosomatic model was consequently abandoned.

In conclusion, the conventional medical model was upheld by the data and the rival psychosomatic hypothesis failed to be supported. While both models were plausible, the better-fitting model is perhaps easier to interpret. When cardiac patients continue to feel chest pain after undergoing an apparently successful operation, it is not surprising that they become discouraged and that their state of well-being is affected. An individual who is often in low spirits and who is pessimistic and defeatist is

Figure 4.6
Quality-of-Life Model for Cardiac Patients

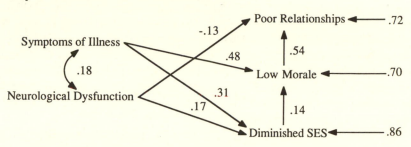

Source: From "A Structural Analysis of Health-related Quality of Life Dimensions" by D. M. Romney, C. D. Jenkins, & J. M. Bynner, 1992, *Human Relations, 45,* p. 172. Copyright 1992 by Plenum Publishing Corporation. Reprinted by permission.

not good company and is likely to lose contact with friends and relatives. Moreover, because of the patient's physical and mental (easily fatigued) condition, he or she is unlikely to be as efficient in their job as they were before and may have to transfer to a less-demanding and less-well-paid job, which would further lower morale. Because this model supports the notion that the physical and mental symptoms associated with the heart condition and the heart surgery have a detrimental effect on the individual's quality of life rather than the other way round, the best way to ameliorate the situation would appear to be to use medical means to control these symptoms. Failing that, an attempt should be made to boost the patient's morale via supportive psychotherapy.

Figure 4.7
Alternative Quality-of-Life Model for Cardiac Patients

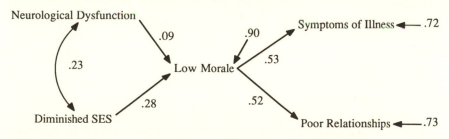

Source: From "A Structural Analysis of Health-related Quality of Life Dimensions" by D. M. Romney, C. D. Jenkins, & J. M. Bynner, 1992, *Human Relations, 45,* p. 172. Copyright 1992 by Plenum Publishing Corporation. Reprinted by permission.

DISCUSSION AND CONCLUSIONS

The examples we have considered in this chapter of various kinds of self-attitude measures and their relations among themselves and with other variables extend the sort of reasoning advanced in previous chapters. To understand fully the way in which the self-concept is formed and how it influences other attitudes and behavior, we need to develop models that allow these variables to interact dynamically and mutually reinforce each other. The traditional hierarchical model of attitude structure is unable to entertain this possibility, presenting the self-concept as a relatively fixed entity reflecting deeper personality traits and affected only marginally by influences from outside.

The causal models developed here are in line with a more process-oriented conception (e.g., Bandura 1982; Markova 1987). They suggest an alternative and much more useful way of conceptualizing self-image data, which leads directly to strategies for producing change. Thus at the heart of teenage identity lies positive or negative evaluation, which itself underpins other, more specific forms of emotional states such as lack of self-confidence, fatalism, depression, alienation, and weakened motivation. At the end of the sequence, such consequences as poor school performance and delinquency are likely to arise either directly or via hostile attitudes directed outwards at the institutions of society such as politics. What damages self-esteem will typically be negative appraisal in the eyes of others.

Thus, for adolescents, success in the domains of education and social life is likely to be critically important in ensuring that the key tasks in adult identity formation (Erikson 1968; Hendry 1989) are achieved successfully. The findings from the health-related quality-of-life data extended the conclusions into adulthood itself, looking at cases in which identity is challenged by the traumatic effects of serious illness. For the cardiac patients in the last study discussed, it is the effect of physical symptoms that produces negative self-appraisals from others; the debilitating process of illness jeopardizes occupational position, and this leads to lower morale and poorer relationships. The process operates predominantly in one direction. Though we may expect some aggravation of symptoms from poor relationships, the symptoms themselves lie at the heart of the problem. The prime target for therapy should, therefore, be to alleviate the symptoms.

Although we have tended to focus on the dominant direction of influence indicated by our best-fitting models, we acknowledge that all of the processes described, especially those concerned with teenage identity, are probably cyclical in nature. Unsatisfactory performance in the school, peer group, or hospital, or presumably in the workplace too, is seen to be at the core of "threatened identity" (Breakwell 1986). This deficit in performance is itself likely to be reinforced and perpetuated through the effects of negative appraisal. If the individual takes no action to break the circle by finding other means of restoring self-esteem, his or her difficulties are likely to be compounded. Teachers and therapists can play a crucial part in helping to arrest the process, because the way they react to the individual's performance will be central in the formation of the individual's negative self-perceptions. In the following chapter we shall consider general strategies of intervention that might be most effectively employed.

It should be obvious from this chapter that the models vary in complexity with the domain being examined. Abilities can be modeled by straightforward simplexes and personality traits can be modeled by a circumplex; but attitudes require more complex models than do either abilities or personality traits. Thus one self-attitude in a linear sequence is not only influenced by the attitude preceding it and exercises an influence on the attitude immediately following it, but it may also influence other attitudes in the linear sequence.

There are risks, of course, in placing too much weight on some of these pathways; we know that any model-fitting exercise runs the risk of capitalizing on chance. Justification for including pathways in the model needs, therefore, to be based on sound theory and on the evidence from replication. In the examples quoted here, the models can be supported on both of these grounds. The models lend support to well-developed theoretical positions in the social-learning and social-process traditions of identity study; they also have stability across replications in different samples. We may therefore feel confident that they offer a sound basis for self-attitude change.

Chapter 5

Implications and Applications

In this final chapter the factor- versus structural model debate will be revisited in the context of the findings from our studies described in the previous chapters. Our *motif* that alternative structures to the common-factor model should always be considered will continue to be emphasized. Some psychologists (e.g., Kail & Pellegrino 1985) are inclined to believe that the psychometric approach has reached a dead end because it fails to take into account the processes that underlie mental acts. We would argue, however, that the psychometric approach, if it now moves in the direction that we have been advocating, should be able to shed some light on how these processes operate on one another.

Using SEM as an alternative to FA, we believe that we have made a number of interesting discoveries; in this chapter we will indicate how these discoveries may contribute substantively to theory and practice. In all domains, we have found that personal characteristics can be modeled *dynamically* so that a change in one characteristic can be conceived as producing a change in another. This is certainly true in the case of cognitive abilities, where vocabulary can be seen to govern two separate ability strands, one verbal, the other numerical. The importance of vocabulary for the growth of cognitive skills, therefore, becomes recognized as paramount. The findings from our research on personality disorders are more complicated, half of the disorders lying on a straight line (simplex) and half lying on a circle (circumplex). The simplex traces the development of conscience and conscientiousness; the circumplex shows how interpersonal personality traits overlap with and complement one another. Both models suggest that personality change can be readily achieved by appropriate intervention. In our analysis of attitudes toward self in young people, low self-esteem is seen to initiate chains of self-deprecating attitudes that lead eventually to low attainment and to political estrangement. Fortunately, this downward spiral is not inevitable, and many strategies for enhancing self-esteem in children and youth are now available (e.g., Battle 1987, 1989). Personal characteristics, whether they be intellectual, behavioral, or attitudinal, are all amenable to change. This is the message that the findings from our research constantly convey.

With regard to methodology, we shall be reflecting later in this chapter on the implications of SEM for validity and reliability and for causation and parsimony. SEM is, of course, no panacea. The internal validity of research conclusions has to be judged by the extent to which alternative explanations of research results can be ruled out. In this sense, experimental controls will always set the standard by which causal interpretations need to be judged; wherever feasible these should be employed alongside SEM. Moreover, there are a number of methodological problems with SEM that still have to be resolved, such as deciding upon the best index for assessing goodness-of-fit. Some of the outstanding methodological issues will be raised later in this chapter.

The remainder of the chapter will be devoted first to discussing applications of our findings in the fields of education, mental health, and citizenship training, and second to outlining a prospective research program. We believe that SEM has an important role to play in the future, not only in building and testing theories, but also as an adjunct to other research agendas currently developing with which we have sympathy.

IMPLICATIONS FOR THEORY AND PRACTICE

Intelligence

As we have seen, theories of personal characteristics have been rooted in the pervasive notion that abilities, traits, and attitudes are fixed quantities that limit human beings' capacity to learn. This notion is consistent with the belief that abilities are inherited and therefore predetermined. The "discovery of factors" through factor analysis has been taken as evidence by the proponents of the hereditary approach that they are right. The implications of this viewpoint are far-reaching.

Ever since the days of Herbert Spencer and Francis Galton, intelligence had been viewed as a biological characteristic. Recently Eysenck (1986) defined intelligence as "the biological fundament of cognitive processing, genetically based (perhaps entirely so), responsible for individual differences in intellectual competence" (1). The factor *g* discovered by Spearman is believed by the followers of this school of thought to represent the general intelligence with which an individual is born and which intelligence tests attempt to measure. As intelligence represents the ability to achieve, how well a person achieves will be limited by this ability. Those who perform below their level of ability used to be designated "underachievers," whereas those who perform above this level were once called "overachievers." The very term "overachiever" has fallen into disuse, however, for good reason—it implied that the individual was somehow exceeding his or her potential by trying too hard!

The unfortunate concept of overachievement is predicated on the belief that intelligence is somehow fixed and inert. We have, however, demonstrated via SEM that cognitive abilities need not be attributed to the underlying common factor we call "intelligence" but can be better explained in terms of a dynamic split-simplex structure; that is, a linear sequence of abilities with one ability leading to and enhancing another. In the forefront of the structure is vocabulary. The split simplex tells us that, if we increase children's vocabulary, the improvement should flow down the line and result in an improvement in their other linguistic skills and also in their numerical skills.

In the normal population, all children learn a language with ease, but those who are socially and educationally disadvantaged are unlikely to have the rich vocabulary and semantic competence of the others. Those children will almost certainly perform badly on intelligence tests that involve the use of standard English. Instead of interpreting these findings as an indication that they are "unintelligent" and incapable of benefiting from an education, however, we should recognize the fact that people have different ways of communicating, depending on their upbringing and cultural background, and that what they lack is not innate ability but opportunity. Ironically, the work of Dyer (1970), reported by Jensen (1980) in support of the factor-analytic theories of intelligence, actually shows that practice with mental tasks produces a greater rate of improvement in performance in black (verbally impoverished) homes than in white (verbally enriched) ones.

In chapter 2 we cited the work of Feuerstein, who has successfully adopted a remedial approach with children who are "developmentally disabled," children who in previous times might have been condemned with the epithet "ineducable." The success of his approach challenges the belief that abilities are constrained by centralized cognitive controls limiting what children are able to achieve. The view promoted by Feuerstein and others that intelligence is malleable is one that forces educators to find out what experiences are most likely to assist a student in achieving particular educational goals. If a student is struggling with the basic arithmetical operations, what specific form of instruction will help the child most? The predictive value of tests thereby ceases to be a primary concern; the main criterion for evaluating a test becomes its *diagnostic* value. As Howe concluded:

Practitioners in education have been, and continue to be, misled by preconceived ideas which dictate that intelligence must underlie a child's capabilities. For instance, accepted wisdom dictates the erroneous belief that one child will inevitably fail to gain a particular skill because he is not in possession of sufficient intelligence. There are obvious dangers in any educational policy that is based upon a faulty conceptualization which holds that children's capacities to learn are limited by central constraints which may in fact be illusory. (1990, 493)

We must acknowledge that both cognitive and developmental psychologists base their interpretations of intelligence on different assumptions. The former have focused on uncovering the processes by which individuals solve test items, and the latter have studied how the mental capacity of children develops systematically with the result that performance improves. To predict that children will do poorly at school based on their current IQs and then to sit back and wait for this to happen is self-defeating. In support of this position, our own research endorses the view that a more favorable outcome is possible. Such an outcome must be actively fostered by intervening with the appropriate instruction, based on what we know of the children's strengths and weaknesses.

Personality

The same remarks we have made about the alleged fixity of intelligence could also be made in relation to personality. By definition, personality is considered to be stable and enduring: "The leopard does not change his spots, nor the Abyssinian his skin." The popularity of the Big Five dimensions of personality does nothing to dispel this belief. The alternative structures of personality, on the other hand, as exemplified by the circumplex and simplex models which we found to apply to personality disorders, give rise to some optimism. These structures inspire hope that the extreme and rigid behaviors manifested by those individuals diagnosed with personality disorders are amenable to change. The advent of interpersonal psychotherapy, strongly influenced by the circumplex theory of personality, has provided us with a powerful tool for treating these disorders and for bringing about the desired personality change. Our own discovery that not all personality disorders lie on a circle but that half lie on a straight line or simplex has other implications for treatment. In the latter disorders, the main problem seems to be impaired cognitive style rather than disturbed interpersonal relationships. The treatment of choice for these particular disorders appears, therefore, to be cognitive therapy rather than interpersonal therapy. In sum, SEM has revealed an important finding vis-à-vis the treatment of a major subset of personality disorders. It is precisely its power to discover and verify a model of functional relationships with implications for action that makes SEM so useful.

In chapter 3 we also discussed how the paranoid process develops in those individuals who are afflicted. This process can be depicted by a simplex representing the stages they pass through as the disorder becomes more severe. What is interesting, however, is not so much the natural course of the disorder as the strength of the links between the sequential stages. Our findings indicated that the links at the end of chain, where paranoid delusions start to appear, are weaker than those at the beginning. This suggests that delusions may not be held with the unshakable conviction that has traditionally been their hallmark and that they are not impervious to psychotherapy. Indeed, we supplied evidence from two studies that showed how patients, subjected to the appropriate psychological treatment, could be freed from delusions that had troubled them for years. The findings from SEM, therefore, point the way to a treatment objective that in the past would have been considered unobtainable but that is currently high on the agenda. In contrast, the FA approach, with its identification of a single underlying paranoid factor, has no treatment utility whatsoever.

The noteworthy feature of the circumplex and simplex models of personality is that they imply the ability to *change*. Personality is ordered on a continuum. Personality traits blend into one another either around a circle or on a straight line, depending on which traits we are talking about. Furthermore, the way in which the personality traits are arranged has particular implications for therapy. One particularly successful form of treatment that can be linked to the circumplex model of personality is *assertiveness training*. Some individuals, mainly women, are both passive and dependent; they rely on others to make their decisions for them and are too timid to say "no" when asked to do something they prefer not to do. Such individuals may have been dominated by their parents since childhood and conditioned to act in a subservient manner. They may also be afraid to "stand up for their rights" for fear they may estrange the people on whom they depend for their livelihood or emotional sustenance. The goal of treatment in such cases should be to induce a shift in interpersonal behavior away from the kind of behavior characterized by the personality trait on the periphery of the circle towards the complementary kind of behavior characterized by the personality trait diametrically opposite. Psychotherapy in such cases would probably consist of (1) giving clients insight into their condition; (2) restructuring their cognitions so that they no longer believe that asserting themselves appropriately will lead to disaster; and (3) getting them to practice asserting themselves by role-playing situations with the therapist or with "confederates," so-called behavior rehearsal. Although these specific therapeutic techniques may not stem directly from circumplex theory, the thrust of the therapy is very much in line with the theory's tenets that change is possible and that people can "balance" their personalities by acquiring those traits that are complementary.

Self-concept

The dominant tradition of attitude research has adopted a dimensional model to represent attitudes. Use of factor analysis to identify basic attitudes has led to a hierarchical classification along the lines of those of ability and personality with raw opinions ultimately residing in more fundamental (higher level) predispositions such as authoritarianism and radicalism versus conservatism. Attitudes toward the self have also been studied with the aid of factor analysis; and factors corresponding to the "self-concept," "self-esteem," and "self-efficacy" have been identified.

Self-attitudes play a very important part in the lives of teenagers. Teenagers who perform inadequately at school develop a poor self-concept in relation to their ability to do academic work; that is, they have low self-efficacy. The model indicates that, if this state of affairs is not remedied, the result could lead to a drop in self-esteem, then a sense of alienation, and then an emergence of delinquent behavior. Similarly, educational attainment may be impaired when diminished self-esteem leads in turn to depression, lowered self-confidence, and reduced motivation. But motivation underpins educational attainment, and low attainment is the main reason for loss of self-esteem in the first place.

What is needed is for teachers to intervene at an early stage to prevent the student from embarking on these vicious circles. Cognitive-behavioral techniques for improving self-efficacy (first formulated by Bandura) have been mentioned in a previous chapter. According to our structural model, the application of these techniques with children who are at risk, frequently those from lower socioeconomic groups, is a necessity if we are to avert a negative outcome. The common-factor model postulated to explain the relationships among the four variables—self-concept school ability, self-esteem, anomie, and delinquency—does not indicate what steps we should take to ameliorate the situation though it does suggest that self-esteem plays a central role.

A further example to illustrate the point that SEM may have greater utility for intervention than FA concerns the relationship between self-esteem and depression. It is a well-established fact that the two are inversely related. What is of interest to mental health workers is that a drop in self-esteem seems to *precede* depression rather than the other way round. We demonstrated this finding quite clearly with SEM when analyzing the data from the 16–19 Initiative. The common-factor model, which proposed an underlying self-esteem factor to account for the correlation between the two variables, did not fit so well as the structural model and was consequently discounted.

The superiority of the structural model over the factor model is that it provides a definite recommendation for intervention; in this case, the recommendation is to help young people who are depressed and suffering from low self-esteem by intervening to raise their self-esteem. Of course, not everyone who is depressed also has low self-esteem; the depression may be a reaction to external events such as a death in the family. But in cases where the two conditions coincide, depression is a function of lowered self-esteem. In clinical situations, rational-emotive therapy by

Ellis (Ellis, Bernard, & DiGiuseppe 1988) and cognitive therapy by Beck (1987) are two of the mainstays for treating these conditions. Essentially, both therapies involve disproving the false beliefs and assumptions that people hold about themselves and the way they are perceived by others that make them devalue their own worth. The alternative form of therapy to lift the individual's mood with, say, antidepressive medication, cannot provide more than a temporary relief because the cause of the problem, the low self-esteem, will remain untouched. Similarly, because we tend to value school performance most of all in education, children who do poorly have nothing else to fall back on to preserve their self-esteem. In these cases, we need to reinforce other activities to maintain their self-esteem. Once again we see how SEM can put us on the right track, whereas FA cannot.

In our health-related quality-of-life study, the common-factor model merely indicates that quality of life could be regarded as a second-order factor accounting for the intercorrelations among the primary factors. It does not signal any particular course of action to enhance quality of life. Our structural model, on the other hand, is quite definite in its implications. First and foremost, we need to alleviate patients' symptoms. This will boost their morale, which will in turn improve their interpersonal relationships. In other words, to enrich the quality of life of patients with health problems, the first step is to mitigate the symptoms of their illness. This is an important finding insofar as it suggests that trying to do it the other way round (i.e., first improving their interpersonal relationships) is doomed to failure. Thus we see from these two examples the usefulness of SEM, as opposed to FA, in making decisions about the most effective intervention.

IMPLICATIONS FOR METHODOLOGY

Reliability and Validity

Factor analysis is useful for establishing homogeneous sets of items to form unidimensional scales. These scales are more reliable than the individual items that compose them, because the random-error variance associated with the items tends to be canceled out. In other words, factor analysis corrects for attenuation by grouping together similar items. Whatever is being measured by the scale is identified from the nature of the items themselves, especially those that have high factor loadings. But this does not necessarily mean that what is being measured by the scale has any substantive significance. In SEM, however, we can determine how a factor relates functionally to other factors within a theoretical framework; that is, we can test the validity of the components of a particular model. An example from data considered earlier demonstrates the distinction between reliability and validity in SEM terms and shows how the form of the model can affect reliability and validity estimates.

A tradition has grown of using factor analysis to establish the construct validity of psychological tests and then of designating the loadings as "validity coefficients" (Andrews 1982; Heise & Bohrnstedt 1970). In these terms, under SEM the choice between different models to account for a set of correlations among variables can produce quite different reliability and validity estimates. If we take another look at the analysis of the Richmond Tests of Basic Skills described in chapter 2, we see that a simplex interpretation of a set of indicators of verbal ability can lead to radically different conclusions about reliability and validity than those arrived at by the factor model. Table 5.1 presents validities and reliabilities for the six subtests under the different measurement models applied to these data. The table gives the validity and reliability coefficient in each case for each indicator, and also below each column of coefficients gives the goodness-of-fit ratio, χ^2/df (from Bynner 1990).

As we move from four to five variables, we see small but clear shifts in the size of the validities, more accentuated, of course, for the reliabilities (shown in parentheses). In addition, the fit is relatively poor for all these models, even though cursory inspection of the correlation matrix would lead most experienced factor analysts using exploratory methods to conclude that a single-factor solution was the appropriate one. The fit of all the models is poor, the best being for the six-indicator model (lowest χ^2 ratio).

Further improvements in the fit for this model can be achieved by including residual correlations (i.e., correlations between the errors in the model). As noted earlier, these may either be interpreted as method effects or as representing additional constructs measured by the indicators. We see immediately that large reductions in the χ^2 ratio occur even when only one such residual correlation is included in the model. As residual correlations are introduced, we also see substantial changes in the validities, some increasing and others decreasing.

Finally, in the last column on the right of the table, we have the figures for reliability and validity obtained in the simplex model. Here, quite different levels of validity are indicated, with substantial improvements being achieved in most cases. Again, the fit of the model to the data is excellent, as good as the comparable factor model with four residual correlations included.

This empirical example demonstrates how the choice of theoretical model can have a dramatic effect on some validity and reliability estimates and less effect on others. Yet the traditional idea of a validity and particularly of a reliability coefficient is that it is a property inherent in

Table 5.1
Validities and Reliabilities Under Different Models

Indicator	one factor 4 variable	one factor 5 variable	one factor 6 variable	+res* r_{12}	+res* r_{12} r_{45}	+res* r_{12} r_{45} r_{36}	+res* r_{12} r_{45} r_{36} r_{23}	Simplex with optimum order 1,2,6,3,4,5
1.	.84(.71)	.81(.66)	.80(.64)	.74(.73)	.75(73)	.74(.73)	.74(.72)	.91(.83)
2.	.88(.77)	.85(.73)	.85(.73)	.80(.82)	.81(.83)	.79(.80)	.81(.87)	.91(.83)
3.	.76(.58)	.80(.64)	.80(.84)	.82(.67)	.82(.67)	.85(.79)	.86(.86)	.84(.71)
4.	.72(.52)	.76(.58)	.76(.58)	.79(.62)	.77(.69)	.76(.67)	.75(.66)	.82(.67)
5.	—	.73(.53)	.73(.53)	.76(.58)	.74(.62)	.73(.62)	.72(.62)	.82(.67)
6.	—	—	.81(.66)	.81(.66)	.82(.67)	.85(.80)	.85(.80)	.84(.71)
X^2	105	210	213	53	34	17	8	9.5
df	2	5	9	8	7	6	5	6
$\dfrac{X^2}{df}$	52.5	42	23.7	6.6	4.9	2.8	1.6	1.6

*+res means that residual correlations such as r_{12} are included in the model (6 variable). Reliabilities are shown in brackets.

the instrument itself rather than something that is dependent on the theoretical context in which it is applied.

Construct Validation

To equate a factor with a construct and then to equate "factorial validity" with construct validity is to show a faulty understanding of the process of construct validation (Bynner 1988). Pawson (1980) points out that a *necessary* condition for construct validity is not the same as a *sufficient* condition. Factor loadings should really not be interpreted as validity coefficients but as reliability coefficients analogous to Cronbach's coefficient α (Cronbach 1951). Factor analysis is basically a *classificatory* mechanism making possible the groupings of similar items into a composite measure that *de facto* will be more reliable than the items themselves; that is, FA is a way of correcting for attenuation. Just because factors are descriptive aggregates of related variables does not mean that they have real significance. As Anastasi (1983) remarked: "They are not underlying entities or causal factors, but descriptive categories" (372). Although high intercorrelations among, say, ability measures become a necessary condition for validating the intelligence construct, correlation itself clearly fails to provide sufficient evidence that the tests are measuring the same phenomenon (i.e., that there is a latent construct underlying them), for there are many equally legitimate ways of explaining the correlations. And as Cronbach and Meehl (1955) put it in their original account of construct validation: "The integration of diverse data into a proper interpretation cannot be an entirely quantitative process" (300). The theoretical status of a postulated construct and hence the validity of its measurement must depend on other sources of evidence, empirical as well as conceptual, not just on the correlation alone.

In order to show that a given construct applies to a test, it is necessary to derive hypotheses about test behavior from theory related to the construct and verify them experimentally. The theory of anxiety . . . might include such expectations as . . . anxiety increases when subjects are subjected to a threat of electric shock; neurotics are more anxious than nonneurotics; anxiety is lowered by a certain drug; anxious persons set high goals for themselves. Each of these expectations can be tested by an experiment or statistical study (Cronbach 1970, 123).

Whenever these expectations are confirmed, the construct anxiety is cross validated. Construct validity is much more complex than the other kinds of validity. It is not enough to show that different measures of anxiety—self-rating scales, ratings by others, psychophysiological monitoring, and avoidant behavior—all converge and will, when factorized, produce a single factor. One has to demonstrate empirically a "nomological network" of laws expressing the functional properties of the construct in relation to other constructs and the observations used to measure them. Although sophisticated SEM techniques for analyzing multitrait-multimethod matrices may produce factor loadings of a trait on its measure that are uncontaminated by the effects of other traits or by the methods of measurement, to label these factor loadings as "construct validity coefficients" is presumptuous. Establishing the existence of a factor quantitatively is merely the first step, albeit an important one. It should be clear by now that construct validation is an ongoing process analogous to theory construction and cannot be achieved through statistical analysis alone. This point is emphasized in an illuminating article by Embretson (1983) in which she discusses both "construct representation" (the identification of the theoretical mechanisms that underlie task performance) and "nomothetic span" (the network of relationships of a test to other measures).

SEM and Causation

The strongest claim a scientist can make about a set of data is that one variable is caused by another. Until recently it was rare for an investigator to make that claim solely on the basis of correlational data. Recently, however, causal modeling employing statistical controls has become commonplace, although the *a priori* assumptions that must be met to reach the crucial decision that a relationship is not spurious . . . are, in practice, seldom if ever met by the social scientists who use these techniques. (Baumrind 1983, 1295)

It is a truism that correlation does not imply causation. Most correlations are probably casual rather than causal. However, as Cliff (1983) warned us, the language of SEM may trap the naive researcher into thinking that causes have been established when a structural model fits the data when what should be concluded is that *possible causal explanations have been ruled out*. Despite Cliff's timely warning, there still exists the mistaken belief that causation can be proved by means of SEM. For example, Leong, Cheng, Lundberg, Olofsson, and Mulcahy (1989) state: "The structural equation modelling overcomes the possible objection that correlation does not necessarily imply causation in that each equation in the model represents a 'causal' link rather than a mere association" (17).

Causal modeling is more correctly referred to as *the modeling of causal hypotheses*.

As long as social scientists find it useful to think of one thing as influencing, bringing about, effecting, determining, or causing another, there is no reason to abandon causal statements. Despite the philosopher's unease with statements of causation, and the statistician's insistence that there is nothing causal about equations, social scientists are free to judge the utility of thinking causally about their data sets, and to exploit the consistencies between structural equations and causal thinking. (Hayduk 1987, xv–xvi)

Causation can be demonstrated only through experimentation where the direct influence of the independent variable on the dependent variable can be isolated by controlling for extraneous variables that may have an effect on the dependent variable. In other words, demonstration of causal effects depends on the "internal validity" of the research design (Campbell & Stanley 1963; Cook & Campell 1979). If manipulation of the independent variable produces a change in the dependent variable and if this change cannot be ascribed to the influence of any other variable besides the independent variable in question, then we can safely conclude that the change in the independent variable causes a change in the dependent variable. The chief advantage of the experimental method is that it gives us strong grounds for attributing causation. Other methods (e.g., surveys) that can demonstrate that variables are associated allow much weaker inferences because, as we have seen, there is no unique way to model the correlations. The confidence with which we prefer one model to another then depends on logical considerations, such as temporality and theoretical consistency. So first we need to have a viable causal hypothesis to model.

In chapter 1 we discussed how a correlation between two variables may be interpreted via four different models: (1) a recursive-path model from A to B; (2) a recursive-path model from B to A; (3) a common-factor model; or (4) a nonrecursive- or reciprocal-path model. These four models all make some very restrictive assumptions about the data. They ignore residuals and any relationships that might exist between them; they do not mix different forms of functional relationships; and they are, of course, all linear models. Retaining the linearity assumption but dispensing with the others, the set of models depicted below gives some idea of the great variety of interpretations that can be placed upon a simple correlation (see Figure 5.1). Note again that none of these models corresponds to the single-factor model. Only model 3a approaches it, but in this model the correlation between the residuals suggests that the indicators are not unidimensional and that they share more than one factor.

Why is it then that, when confronted with a set of correlated tests or other measures, we turn almost compulsively to just one of the possible models, the common-factor model? Regardless of how we have designed our measures to operationalize a given construct, the mere evidence of correlation is not sufficient to prove its existence. Rigorous theoretical analysis backed by a range of empirical evidence from naturalistic observation to controlled experiments are the essential counterparts of correlational data. Correlations should be viewed, not as a means of discovering

Figure 5.1
Models of Bivariate Correlation Including Relations Between Residuals

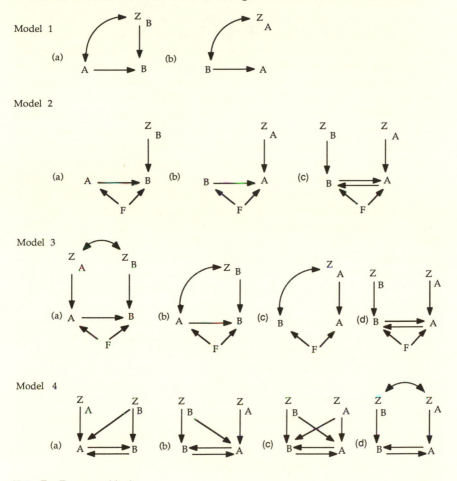

Note: Z_A, Z_B are residuals.

Source: From "Factor Analysis and the Construct Indicator Relationship" by J. M. Bynner, 1988, *Human Relations, 41,* p. 39. Copyright 1988 by Plenum Publishing Corporation. Reprinted by permission.

structure and consequently theory, but as an appropriate tool for evaluating one theoretically derived structure against another. This, however, should not rule out the use of the results of any one evaluation to modify or improve a given model. Exploration and confirmation go hand in hand in theory construction, underpinned along the way by replication.

MODELING AND THE PARSIMONY PRINCIPLE

The fourteenth-century English philosopher and theologian William of Occam formulated the principle of parsimony known as Occam's Razor. According to this principle, "entities are not to be multiplied except as may be necessary." This was applied by the nineteenth-century animal psychologist Lloyd Morgan, whose famous "canon" specified that we should not attribute to animals human properties in order to explain their behavior, which he regarded as instinctive. In other words, theories should be kept as simple as possible. If two competing theories have equal explanatory power and equal empirical support, the simpler of the two— the one with fewer assumptions and suppositions—should be adopted, even if the other hypothesis currently holds sway. This principle has been endorsed by many influential scientists ever since (e.g., Heinrich Hertz, Henri Poincaré, and George Mead, to name but a few). Most recently the celebrated psychological statistician Jacob Cohen (1990) has added his weight to this school of thought ("I have also learnt that simple is better," 1304). Indeed, the whole tradition of factor analysis, which is based on the proposition that there are fewer factors than the variables from which they are derived (Thurstone 1947), is consistent with the parsimony principle. Although Occam never explained the rationale of his principle, perhaps Karl Popper (1934–68) put his finger on it when he declared: "The epistemological questions which can arise in connection with the concept of simplicity can all be answered if we equate this concept with *degree of falsifiability*" (140). What he meant was that it is easier to test and replicate, and therefore fail to confirm, a simple hypothesis than a more complicated one. And science marches on through the confirming or failing to confirm hypotheses.

In choosing between competing models, parsimony is an important and desirable condition. Alternative complex models that may fit the data better could be capitalizing on chance, with the result that their parameter estimates would be unstable. This means that such a model would fail to replicate on another sample. A distinction should be made, however, between models that are parsimonious because they have few *pathways* and represent them in the simplest way possible by linear equations, and models that are parsimonious because they have few *constructs*. When we add pathways to, or subtract pathways from, a given model we are essentially trying out different versions of the same basic model in order to obtain the best fit (i.e., the models are nested within one another). Adding or subtracting constructs, on the other hand, is a much more radical procedure. In adding another construct to a model we are conceding that the theory underlying the previous model is inadequate and that to explain the data properly we need to invoke an additional factor. Social scientists have long recognized the fact that the phenomena they study are multiply determined and that models have to be comprehensive if they are to be of any value. The drive to parsimony, when it leads to insistence on a model with a very limited number of factors, may therefore be counterproductive. In other words, there is a trade-off between simplicity and comprehensiveness.

Perhaps the most outstanding parsimonious account of complex phenomena is Spearman's *g*, which reduces all mental functioning to one single entity. Attractive as this simplicity is, it can, as we have seen, also be misleading. Spearman's *g* factor masks distinction between different types of mental skill, as Thurstone recognized. But even if we add more factors to account for mental performance, we may miss the way in which these performances relate to one another. Therefore, rather than one factor we need many; rather than a factorial account of their origins, we should see them as dynamically related. In this case, sacrificing simplicity for comprehensiveness not only provides a more intrinsically satisfying account but, more importantly, provides a more effective guide to action.

OTHER METHODOLOGICAL ISSUES

With respect to the question of methodology, there are still a number of outstanding issues. The debate about which is the best-fit index is still raging (Mulaik, James, van Alstine, Bennett, Lind, & Stilwell 1989). Although everyone agrees that the original χ^2 statistic is unsatisfactory because it is so dependent on sample size, other measures based on the squared-multiple correlation, such as the goodness-of-fit index, have also shown themselves to be sensitive to sample size (even though they are not supposed to be). Another problem with these fit indices, which compare the model's reproduced covariance matrix to the actual observed covariance matrix, is that they are much more influenced by the measurement portion of the model than by the causal portion. "It is quite possible to have a model in which the measurement portion . . . is correctly specified but in which the causal model portion . . . is misspecified and to still have a goodness-of-fit index for the overall model in the high .80s and .90s" (Mulaik et al. 1989, 440–41).

Indices such as the AGFI (adjusted goodness-of-fit index), which take parsimony into account by compensating for the improvement in fit due to estimating more parameters, are also subject to criticism; for example, the AGFI can assume negative values. Consequently, James, Mulaik, and Brett (1982) have developed their own *parsimony index* by multiplying the normed-fit index (NFI) by the ratio of the degrees of freedom of the hypothesized model to the degrees of freedom of the null model (i.e., the most restrictive model). For instance, in exploratory factor analysis the "null model" would be a model with only zero-factor loadings, so that there are no common factors and the unique variances are equal to the variances of the manifest variables (Bentler & Bonnett 1980). However, in other kinds of analysis the null model may be difficult to decide upon (Sobel & Bohrnstedt 1985), and whether or not the better-fitting model is indeed the better model depends also on the model's interpretability.

The term *specification error* was introduced in chapter 1. This occurs when we specify a model incorrectly and there is a bad fit. Normally, improvements to the model can be accomplished by making the model more complicated. But what of those cases where we specify the model *in*correctly and there is a good fit? This could happen in models where there are negative variances or factor loadings greater than one (so-called Heywood cases). We may then be tempted to keep changing the model until we find one that does fit, and interpret it *post hoc*. This kind of model trimming has come under attack by sociologists (e.g., Cuttance 1985) because it undermines the importance of theory in model construction. The objection to this practice becomes even more apparent when we have a model with a good fit and still go ahead and eliminate the negligible pathways. SEM is not supposed to be conducted on an *ad hoc* basis, although of course we would be burying our heads in the sand if we were to ignore what the data tell us. This issue harkens back to the question of parsimony. Striking a balance between parsimony and complexity is inevitably a subjective process and is, therefore, bound to give rise to disagreements about procedure and interpretation in SEM.

Another controversial issue is the use of cross-sectional data for a model that entails a time sequence, such as the simplex. The problem is that longitudinal surveys containing many repeated measures are often hard to come by, so we must make do with what we have. Secondly, interpreting the meaning of β coefficients in longitudinal research is not straightforward, particularly during periods of development or growth. The β coefficient measures how one variable changes with another, but over time the coefficient itself may change and may no longer be endowed with the stability that we expect from such coefficients. It is as if instead of a using an index to measure speed, we are now using another kind of index, one that measures acceleration. Ragosa and Willett (1985) suggest using individual growth curves as an alternative, but the practicality of that approach remains to be demonstrated, especially when the number of growth points at which data are collected is limited (e.g., Hotchkiss 1979).

The fact that SEM cannot actually prove causality has already been stressed. However, it can be used to *rule out* causal pathways, a very useful function. Nowadays researchers try to avoid the term "causal" in SEM in order not to create a false impression. Personally, we have reverted to talking about the functional relationships between variables, which is, after all, what regression coefficients measure; we refer to their sequential order when appropriate. This might seem like a retrograde step but at least it prevents the uninitiated from mistaking ostensible causes for real causes (cf. Leong et al. 1989).

NEW AGENDAS FOR RESEARCH

It should be clear from what has been said in this chapter that our venture into the use of SEM in the study of personal characteristics is only beginning. Besides the outstanding methodological questions in determining the correct use of the technique, there are broader strategic issues that need to be addressed. These relate to the nature of the models to be evaluated, the scope of research, and the design of studies. We offer some pointers here to the research agenda that is needed.

Perhaps the most difficult question to resolve is the nature of the model to be evaluated. Factor models and SEM models are linear and recursive. We have defended the adoption of the linearity assumption on the grounds of parsimony and stability. But this assumption needs further investigation for the models presented here. The recursive assumption, in all our studies, is more difficult to defend. The recursive model assumes that the direction of causal influence is one way. Nonrecursive models postulate two-way or multiple-way paths, reflecting reciprocal causation. For example, developing vocabulary may partly influence verbal comprehension, but expanded verbal comprehension may also influence vocabulary. As we noted in chapter 1, such possibilities can be modeled by SEM, but they are rarely applied because the models are difficult to identify. They require more data to produce solutions and more complexity in the model through addition of paths and variables involved in nonrecursive relationships. The problem of instability and capitalizing on chance is also accentuated. For these reasons we eschewed nonrecursive models in our own research, recognizing the possible existence of flows of influence in the opposite direction from those presented (i.e., feedback), but concentrating on identifying the dominant direction of influence. This means that our parameter estimates are properly interpreted as reflecting the assumption that "If all the influence went in this direction, then this is what the parameter estimates would be." The use of antecedent variables to "anchor" our simplexes has helped in this aim, but we recognize there is much further to go. An important step to be taken in new research in this area is developing algorithms and rules for modeling nonrecursive relationships and for applying these to the types of data we have employed here.

With respect to the scope of research in personal characteristics, the opportunities and prospects are limitless. We have concentrated on the domains of abilities, personality disorders, and self-attitudes. As we hinted in chapter 4, the wider field of social and political attitudes, complex as it is, could be transformed by the application of SEM. In communications theory we generally need to understand much better the way attitudes develop, form, and reform in response to changes in other attitudes. SEM provides a means of modeling what is happening and of pointing to the ways that are most effective in bringing about change.

Our research on personality has come from an ecological perspective, with an emphasis on disordered personality characteristics that may be susceptible to change. The field of normal personality, how it develops, and how it changes, is also a fruitful one for SEM research. We need to know not only how adjustment is best achieved but also how different types of personal characteristics are likely to influence each other and be influenced by experience in the home, the education system, and the workplace. We also need to know how personalities change in positive directions as well as negative ones in the light of everyday experience.

The main perspective that shines through all our studies, and those that we hope will follow them, is *developmental*. The question of development raises further questions about the age groups we studied and, more importantly, about the stages in the life span where research could be most effectively directed. We would argue that the contexts in which personal characteristics develop and the changes in them that take place at each stage of life should be a further focus of inquiry and that SEM should be applied across all age ranges where data on personal characteristics can be collected. Much of the developmental dynamics that we are seeking to uncover reside in social and cultural experience. Thus, although we might expect the same characteristics to exist in both sexes, in all socioeconomic groups, in all ethnic groups, and in all nations, the strength of the connections and even the structures themselves probably vary. Such questions of stability and change can only be resolved by empirical investigation, so there is a strong case for including comparative studies in the research program.

The agenda we foresee is a full and challenging one, opening up new avenues of inquiry in fields where particular preconceptions have narrowed research horizons in the past. The practice of equating correlations with factors has dominated research on personal characteristics and the action stemming from such research. Thus to enhance our understanding of how personal characteristics form and operate, we need to design outcome studies in education, therapy, and communication that test the implications of the dynamic structures that have been ascertained by SEM. This calls for experimental research that would parallel the correlational research upon which our work was based. With statistical data, there will always be a degree of fuzziness and uncertainty in the conclusions drawn from a single study; hence the need exists for extensive replications within a coordinated research program.

Finally, we must return to the subjects of study: human beings of all ages from every kind of social and cultural background. The message that our research conveys is that potential for development has less to do with the fixed features of an individual's biology than with the experiences that subsequently shape the dynamics of his or her personal characteristics. Our work to date lends support to the general optimism that many practitioners share about favorable outcomes.

References

Adorno, T. W., Frenkel-Brunswick, E., Levinson, D. J., & Sanford, R. N. (1950). *The authoritarian personality*. New York: Harper & Row.

Allport, G. W. (1931). What is a trait of personality? *Journal of Abnormal and Social Psychology,* 25: 368–72.

Allport, G. W. (1935). Attitudes. In C. A. Murchison (Ed.), *A handbook of social psychology,* 3–5. Worcester: Clark University Press.

Allport, G. W., & Odbert, H. S. (1936). Trait-names: A psycho-lexical study. *Psychological Monographs,* 47, no. 211.

American Psychiatric Association (1987). *Diagnostic and statistical manual of mental disorders*. 3rd ed. rev. Washington, D.C.: American Psychiatric Press.

Anastasi, A. (1983). Evolving trait concepts. *American Psychologist,* 38: 175–84.

Andrews, F. M. (1982). *The construct validity and error components of survey measures: Estimates for a structural modeling approach*. Ann Arbor: University of Michigan, Institute for Social Research.

Bachman, J. G., O'Malley, P. M., & Johnston, J. (1978). *Youth in transition (Vol. VI): Adolescence to adulthood—change and stability in the lives of young men*. Ann Arbor: University of Michigan, Institute for Social Research.

Bandura, A. (1977). Self-efficacy towards a unifying theory of behavior change. *Psychological Review,* 84: 191–215.

Bandura, A. (1982). Self-efficacy mechanisms in human agency. *American Psychologist,* 37: 122–47.

Banks, M., Bates, I., Breakwell, G., Bynner, J., Emler, N., Jamieson, L., & Roberts, K. (1991). *Careers and identities*. Milton Keynes, England: Open University Press.

Battle, J. (1987). *9 to 19: Crucial years for self-esteem in children and youth*. Seattle: Special Child Publications.

Battle, J. (1989). *Enhancing self-esteem and achievement*. Edmonton, Canada: James Battle and Associates.

Baumrind, D. (1983). Specious causal attributions in the social sciences: The reformulated stepping-stone theory of heroin use as exemplar. *Journal of Personality and Social Psychology,* 48: 1289–298.

Beck, D. (1987). *Cognitive therapy of depression*. 2nd ed. New York: Guilford.

Bentler, P. M., & Bonnett, D. G. (1980). Significance tests and goodness of fit in the analysis of covariance structures. *Psychological Bulletin,* 88: 588–606.

Bentler, P. M. (1985). *Theory and implementation of EQS: A structural equation program*. Los Angeles: University of California.

Berkman, L. F., & Syme, S. L. (1979). Social networks, host resistance, and mortality: A nine-year follow-up study of Alameda County residents. *American Journal of Epidemiology*, 109: 186–204.

Binet, A., & Simon, T. (1905). Méthodes nouvelles pour le diagnostic du niveau intellectuel des anormaux. *L'Année Psychologique*, 11: 191–244.

Blashfield, R., Sprock, J., Pinkston, K., & Hodgin, J. (1985). Exemplar prototypes of personality disorder diagnoses. *Comprehensive Psychiatry*, 26: 11–21.

Bowers, K. S. (1973). Situationism in psychology: An analysis and critique. *Psychological Review*, 80: 307–36.

Breakwell, G. M. (1986). *Coping with threatened identities*. London: Methuen.

Bynner, J. M. (1969). *The young smoker*. London: HMSO.

Bynner, J. M. (1981). Use of LISREL in the solution to a higher order factor problem in a study of adolescent self image. *Quality and Quantity*, 15: 523–40.

Bynner, J. M. (1987). Theory, data and observational relations: A structural modelling approach. *International Review of Sociology*, 3: 221–48.

Bynner, J. M. (1988). Factor analysis and the construct indicator relationship. *Human Relations*, 41: 389–405.

Bynner, J. M. (1989). *The anchored simplex: Causal inference with survey data*. Paper presented at the meeting of the Research Committee on Methodology, International Sociological Association, Dubrovnik, Yugoslavia.

Bynner, J. M. (1990). Reliability and validity appraisal through structural equation models. *Bulletin de Méthodologie Sociologique*, 28: 41–55.

Bynner, J. M., & Coxhead, P. (1979). Some problems in the analysis of semantic differential data. *Human Relations*, 32: 367–85.

Bynner, J. M., O'Malley, P. M., & Bachman, J. G. (1981). Self-esteem and delinquency revisited. *Journal of Youth and Adolescence*, 10: 407–17.

Bynner, J. M., & Romney, D. M. (1985). LISREL for beginners. *Canadian Psychology*, 26: 43–49.

Bynner, J. M., & Romney, D. M. (1986). Intelligence, fact or artefact: Alternative structures for cognitive abilities. *British Journal of Educational Psychology*, 56: 12–23.

Byrne, D. (1964). Repression-sensitization as a dimension of personality. In B. A. Maher (Ed.), *Progress in experimental psychology research*. Vol. 1: 170–220. New York: Academic Press.

Campbell, D. T., & Stanley, J. C. (1963). *Experimental and quasi-experimental designs for research*. Chicago: Rand McNally.

Candido, C., & Romney, D. (1990). Attributional style in paranoid versus depressed patients. *British Journal of Medical Psychology*, 63: 355–63.

Cantor, N., Smith, E. E., French, R. D., & Mezzich, J. (1980). Psychiatric diagnosis as prototype categorization. *Journal of Abnormal Psychology*, 89: 181–93.

Carmines, E. G., & McIver, J. P. (1981). Analyzing models with unobserved variables: Analysis of covariance structures. In G. W. Bohrnstedt & E. F.

Borgatta (Eds.), *Social measurement: Current issues,* 65–115. Beverly Hills: Sage.

Cattell, R. B. (1943). The description of personality: II. Basic traits resolved into clusters. *Journal of Social and Abnormal Personality,* 38: 476–506.

Cattell, R. B. (1945). The principal trait clusters for describing personality. *Psychological Bulletin,* 42: 129–69.

Cattell, R. B. (1957). *Personality and motivation structure and measurement.* New York: World Books.

Cattell, R. B. (1963). Theory of fluid and crystalized intelligence: A critical experiment. *Journal of Educational Psychology,* 5: 1–22.

Cattell, R. B., Eber, H. W., & Tatsuoka, M. M. (1970). *Handbook for the Sixteen Personality Questionnaire.* 3rd ed. Champaign, IL: Institute of Personality and Ability Testing.

Cliff, N. (1983). Some cautions concerning the applications of causal modeling methods. *Multivariate Behavioral Research,* 18: 115–26.

Cloninger, R. (1987). A systematic method for clinical description and classification of personality variants: A proposal. *Archives of General Psychiatry,* 44: 573–88.

Cloward, R. A., & Ohlin, L. E. (1960). *Delinquency and opportunity.* New York: Free Press.

Cohen, J. (1990). Things I have learnt (so far). *American Psychologist,* 45: 1304–312.

Coleman, J. C. (1974). *Relationships in adolescence.* London: Routledge & Kegan Paul.

Cook, T. D., & Campbell, D. T. (1979). *Quasi-experimentation: Design and analysis issues for field settings.* Chicago: Rand McNally.

Costa, P. T., Jr., & McCrae, R. R. (1985). *The NEO Personality Inventory Manual.* Odessa, FL: Psychological Assessment Resources.

Coxhead, P., & Bynner, J. M. (1981). Factor analysis of semantic differential data. *Quality and Quantity,* 15: 553–67.

Cronbach, L. J. (1951). Coefficient alpha and the internal structure of tests. *Psychometrika,* 16: 297–334.

Cronbach, L. J. (1970). *Essential psychological testing.* 3rd ed. New York: Harper & Row.

Cronbach, L. J., & Meehl, P. E. (1955). Construct validity in psychological tests. *Psychological Bulletin,* 52: 281–302.

Cudeck, R. (1986). A note on structural models for the circumplex. *Psychometrika,* 15: 143–47.

Cuttance, P. (1985). A general structural equation modeling framework for the social and behavioral sciences. In R. B. Smith (Ed.), *A handbook of social science methods.* Vol. 3: 408–63. New York: Praeger.

Dawes, R. M. (1972). *Fundamentals of attitude measurement.* New York: Wiley.

Digman, J. M. (1990). Personality structure: Emergence of the five-factor model. *Annual Review of Psychology,* 41: 417–440.

Digman, J. M., & Inouye, J. (1986). Further specification of the five robust factors of personality. *Journal of Personality and Social Psychology,* 50: 116–23.

Duncan, O. D. (1975). *Introduction to structural equation models.* New York: Academic Press.

Dyer, P. J. (1970). *Effects of test conditions on Negro-White differences in test scores*. Unpublished Ph.D. diss., Columbia University, New York.

Ellis, A. T., Bernard, M. E., & DiGiuseppe, R. (1988). *Inside rational-emotive therapy*. San Diego, CA: Academic Press.

Embretson, S. (1983). Construct validity: Construct representation versus nomothetic span. *Psychological Bulletin*, 93: 179–97.

Endler, N. S., & Magnusson, K. (1976). Toward an interactional psychology of personality. *Psychological Bulletin*, 83: 956–74.

Erikson, E. H. (1968). *Identity, youth and crisis*. New York: Norton.

Eysenck, H. J. (1944). Types of personality—a factorial study of 700 neurotic soldiers. *Journal of Mental Science*, 90: 851–61.

Eysenck, H. J. (1957a). *The dynamics of anxiety and hysteria*. London: Routledge & Kegan Paul.

Eysenck, H. J. (1957b). *The psychology of politics*. London: Routledge & Kegan Paul.

Eysenck, H. J. (1970). *The structure of human personality*. 3rd ed. London: Methuen.

Eysenck, H. J. (1986). The theory of intelligence and the psychophysiology of cognition. In R. J. Sternberg (Ed.), *Advances in the Psychology of Human Intelligence*. Vol. 3: 1–77. Hillsdale, NJ: Erlbaum.

Eysenck, H. J., & Eysenck, S. B. G. (1964). *Manual of the Eysenck Personality Inventory*. London: University of London Press.

Eysenck, H. J., & Eysenck, S. B. G. (1975). *Manual for the Eysenck Personality Questionnaire*. London: Hodder and Stoughton.

Eysenck, S. B. G., & Eysenck, H. J. (1968). The measurement of psychoticism: A study of factor stability and reliability. *British Journal of Social and Clinical Psychology*, 7: 286–94.

Feuerstein, R. (1979). *The dynamic assessment of retarded potential: The learning potential assessment device, theory, instruments and techniques*. Baltimore: University Park Press.

Fiske, D. W. (1949). Consistency of the factorial structures of personality ratings from different sources. *Journal of Abnormal and Social Psychology*, 44: 329–44.

France, N. (1975). *Richmond Tests of Basic Skills, tables of norms*. London: Nelson.

Frances, A., & Widiger, T. A. (1986). Methodological issues in personality disorder diagnosis. In T. Millon & G. L. Klerman (Eds.), *Contemporary directions in psychopathology: Towards the DSM-IV*, 381–400. New York: Guilford.

Freeman, A., Pretzer, J., Fleming, B., & Simon, K. M. (1990). *Clinical applications of cognitive therapy*, 115–304. New York: Plenum.

Galton, F. (1884). *Hereditary genius: An inquiry into its laws and consequences*. New York: Appleton.

Gergen, K. J. (1971). *The concept of self*. New York: Holt, Rinehart and Winston.

Gergen, K. J. (1987). Towards self as relationship. In E. K. Yardley & T. Honess (Eds.), *Self and identity: Psychosocial perspectives*, 53–63. Chichester: Wiley.

Goldberg, L. R. (1981). Language and individual differences: The search for universals in personal lexicons. *Review of Personality and Social Psychology*, 2: 141–65.

Goldberger, A. (1979). Heritability. *Economica*, 46: 323–47.

Gorsuch, R. L. (1983). *Factor analysis*. Hillsdale, NJ: Erlbaum.

Greenblatt, M., Becerra, R. M., & Serafetinides, E. A. (1982). Social networks and mental health: An overview. *American Journal of Psychiatry*, 139: 977–84.

Guilford, J. P. (1975). Factors and factors of personality. *Psychological Bulletin*, 82: 802–14.

Guilford, J. P., & Hoepfner, R. (1971). *The analysis of intelligence*. New York: McGraw-Hill.

Guttman, L. A. (1954). A new approach to factor analysis: The radex. In P. F. Lazarsfeld (Ed.), *Mathematical thinking in the social sciences*, 258–348. Glencoe, IL: Free Press.

Hallworth, H. J. (1965). Dimensions of personality and meaning. *British Journal of Social and Clinical Psychology*, 4: 161–68.

Hammond, S. (1988). *The meaning and measurement of adolescent estrangement*. Unpublished Ph.D. diss., University of Surrey, England.

Harman, H. (1967). *Modern factor analysis*. Chicago: University of Chicago Press.

Harré, R. (1979). *Social being*. Oxford: Blackwell.

Harter, S. (1985). Processes underlying the construction, maintenance, and enhancement of the self-concept in children. In J. Suls & A. Greenwald (Eds.), *Psychological perspectives on the self*. Vol. 3: 137–87. Hillsdale, NJ: Erlbaum.

Hayduk, L. A. (1987). *Structural equation modeling with LISREL: Essentials and advances*. Baltimore: Johns Hopkins University Press.

Heise, D. R., & Bohrnstedt, G. W. (1970). Validity, invalidity and reliability. In E. F. Borgatta (Ed.), *Sociological methods*, 104–29. San Francisco: Jossey Bass.

Hendry, L. B. (1989). The influence of adolescents and peers on adolescent lifestyles and leisure styles. In K. Hurrelmann & U. Engels (Eds.), *The social world of adolescents: International perspectives*, 245–64. New York: Walter de Gruyter.

Hieronymus, S., & Lindquist, E. P. (1967). *Richmond Tests of Basic Skills. Teachers' guide*. London: Nelson.

Hoelter, J. W. (1983). The analysis of covariance structures: Goodness of fit indices. *Sociological Methods and Research*, 11: 325–44.

Horney, K. (1937). *The neurotic personality in our time*. New York: Harcourt Brace.

Horowitz, L. M., & Vitkus, J. (1986). The interpersonal basis of psychiatric symptoms. *Clinical Psychology Review*, 6: 443–69.

Hotchkiss, L. (1979). *Differential equation methodology applied to career decisions and status: Conceptualization and calculation*. Columbus, OH: National Center for Research in Vocational Education (mimeo).

Howe, M. J. A. (1990). Does intelligence exist? *The Psychologist*, 3: 490–93.

Hunt, J. McVicker (1961). *Intelligence and experience.* New York: Ronald Press.

Hurrelmann, K. (1988). *Social structure and personality development.* Cambridge: Cambridge University Press.

Hyler, S. E., & Lyons, M. (1988). Factor analysis of the DSM-III personality disorder clusters: A replication. *Comprehensive Psychiatry,* 29: 304–08.

James, L. R., Mulaik, S. A., & Brett, J. (1982). *Causal analysis: Models, assumptions and data.* Beverly Hills: Sage.

Jenkins, C. D., Jono, R. T., Stanton, B. A., & Stroup, C. A. (1990). The measurement of health-related quality of life: Major dimensions identified by factor analysis. *Social Science and Medicine,* 31: 925–31.

Jenkins, C. D., & Stanton, B. A. (1984). Quality of life as assessed in the Recovery Study. In N. K. Wenger, M. E. Mattson, C. D. Furberg, & J. Elinson (Eds.), *Assessment of quality in clinical trials of cardiovascular therapies,* 266–80. New York: Le Jacq.

Jensen, A. R. (1980). *Bias in mental testing.* New York: Free Press.

Jöreskog, K. G. (1974). Analyzing psychological data by structural analysis of covariance matrices. In D. H. Krantz, R. C. Atkinson, R. D. Luce, & P. Suppes (Eds.), *Contemporary developments in mathematical psychology.* Vol. 2: 1–56. San Francisco: Freeman.

Jöreskog, K. G., & Sörbom, D. (1979). *Advances in factor analysis and structural equation models.* Cambridge, MA: Abt Associates.

Jöreskog, K. G., & Sörbom, D. (1984). *LISREL VI: Analysis of linear structural relationships by maximum likelihood, instrumental variables, and least squares methods* (3rd ed.). Mooresville, IN: Scientific Software.

Jöreskog, K. G., & Sörbom, D. (1989). *LISREL 7: A guide to the program and applications.* 2nd ed. Chicago: SPSS.

Kail, R., & Pellegrino, J. W. (1985). *Human intelligence: Perspectives and prospects.* New York: Freeman.

Kaplan, H. B. (1975). *Self attitudes and deviant behavior.* Pacific Palisades: Goodyear.

Kass, F., Skodol, A. E., Charles E., Spitzer, R. L., & Williams, J. B. W. (1985). Scaled ratings of DSM-III personality disorders. *American Journal of Psychiatry,* 142: 627–30.

Keating, D. P. (1984). The emperor's new clothes: The "new look" in intelligence research. In R. J. Sternberg (Ed.), *Advances in the psychology of human intelligence.* Vol. 2: 1–45. Hillsdale, NJ: Erlbaum.

Kempthorne, O. (1978). Logical, epistemiological and statistical aspects of nature-nurture data interpretation. *Biometrics,* 34: 1–23.

Kiesler, D. J. (1983). The 1982 interpersonal circle: A taxonomy for complementarity in human transactions. *Psychological Review,* 90: 185–214.

Kiesler, D. J. (1986). The 1982 interpersonal circle: An analysis of DSM-III personality disorders. In T. Millon & G. L. Klerman (Eds.), *Contemporary directions in psychopathology: Towards the DSM-IV,* 571–97. New York: Guilford.

LaForge, R. (1977). Interpersonal Check List (ICL). In J. E. Jones & J. W. Pfeiffer (Eds.), *The 1977 annual handbook for group facilitators,* 89–96. LaJolla, CA: University Associates.

Leary, T. F. (1957). *Interpersonal diagnosis of personality: A functional theory and methodology for personality evaluation.* New York: Ronald Press.

Leong, C. K., Cheng, S. C., Lundberg, I., Olofsson, A., & Mulcahy, R. (1989). The effects of cognitive processing, language access on academic performance–linear structural equation modelling. *Scientia Paedagogica Experimentalis,* 26: 15–46.

Likert, R. (1932). A technique for the measurement of attitudes. *Archives of Psychology,* 140: 1–15.

Lorr, M. R. (1964). A simplex of paranoid projection. *Journal of Consulting Psychology,* 28: 378–80.

Lowe, C. F., & Chadwick, P. D. J. (1990). Verbal control of delusions. *Behavior Therapy,* 21: 461–79.

Markova, I. (1987). Knowledge of the self through interaction. In K. Yardley, & T. Honess (Eds.), *Self and identity: Psychosocial perspectives,* 65–80. Chichester, U.K.: Wiley.

Marsh, A. (1977). *Protest and political consciousness.* London: Sage.

Marsh, H. W., Balla, J. R., & McDonald, R. P. (1988). Goodness of fit indices in confirmatory factor analysis. *Psychological Bulletin,* 103: 391–411.

Matza, D. (1964). *Delinquency and draft.* New York: Wiley.

McClelland, D. C., Atkinson, J. W., Clark, R. A., & Lowell, E. L. (1953). *The achievement motive.* New York: Appleton-Century-Crofts.

McCrae, R. R., & Costa, P. T. (1985). Updating Norman's "adequate taxonomy": Intelligence and personality dimensions in natural language and in questionnaires. *Journal of Personality and Social Psychology,* 49: 710–21.

McDonald, R. P. (1980). A simple comprehensive model for the analysis of covariate structures. *British Journal of Mathematical and Statistical Psychology,* 33: 161–83.

McKennell, A. C. (1970). Attitude measurement: Use of coefficient alpha with cluster or factor analysis. *Sociology,* 4: 227–45.

Mischel, W. (1968). *Personality assessment.* New York: Wiley.

Mulaik, S. A., James, L. R., van Alstine, J., Bennett, N., Lind, S., & Stilwell, C. D. (1989). Evaluation of goodness-of-fit indices for structural equation models. *Psychological Bulletin,* 105: 430–45.

Murray, H. A. (1938). *Explorations in personality.* New York: Oxford University Press.

Norman, W. T. (1963). Toward an adequate taxonomy of personality attributes: Replicated factor structure in peer nomination personality ratings. *Journal of Abnormal and Social Psychology,* 66: 574–78.

Nunnally, J. C. (1978). *Psychometric theory.* New York: McGraw-Hill.

Oppenheim, A. N. (1966). *Questionnaire design and attitude measurement.* London: Heinemann.

Osgood, C. E., Suci, G. T., & Tannenbaum, P. H. (1957). *The measurement of meaning.* Urbana: University of Illinois Press.

Pawson, R. (1980). Empiricist measurement strategies: A critique of the multiple indicator approach to measurement. *Quality and Quantity,* 14: 651–78.

Piaget, J. (1983). *The psychology of intelligence.* Totowa, NJ: Littlefield Adams.

Popper, K. R. (1968). *The logic of scientific discovery.* 3rd ed. London: Hutchinson. (Original work published in 1934.)

Ragosa, D. R., & Willett, J. B. (1985). Understanding correlates of change by modeling individual differences in growth. *Psychometrika,* 50: 203–28.

Richardson, K., & Bynner, J. M. (1984). Intelligence: Past and future. *International Journal of Psychology,* 19: 499–526.

Rokeach, M. (1968). *Beliefs, attitudes and values.* New York: Worth.

Romney, D. M. (1987). A simplex model of the paranoid process: Implications for diagnosis and prognosis. *Acta Psychiatrica Scandinavica,* 75: 651–55.

Romney, D. M., & Bynner, J. M. (1989). Evaluation of a circumplex model of DSM-III personality disorders. *Journal of Research in Personality,* 23: 525–38.

Romney, D. M., & Bynner, J. M. (1992). A simplex model of five DSM-III personality disorders. *Journal of Personality Disorders,* 6: 34–39.

Romney, D. M., Jenkins, C. D., & Bynner, J. M. (1992). A structural analysis of health-related quality of life dimensions. *Human Relations,* 45: 165–76.

Rosch, E. (1978). Principles of categorization. In E. Rosch & B. B. Lloyd (Eds.), *Cognition and categorization.* Hillsdale, NJ: Erlbaum.

Rosenberg, M. (1965). *Society and the adolescent self-image.* Princeton, NJ: Princeton University Press.

Rotter, J. B. (1966). Generalized expectancies for internal versus external control of reinforcement. *Psychological Monographs,* 80, no. 609.

Rudden, M., Gilmore, M., & Frances, A. (1982). Delusions: When we confront the facts of life. *American Journal of Psychiatry,* 139: 929–32.

Saris, W. E., & Stronkhorst, L. H. (1984). *Causal modelling in non-experimental research: An introduction to the LISREL approach.* Amsterdam: Sociometric Research Foundation.

Sherer, M., Maddux, J. E., & Mercandante, B. (1982). The Self-efficacy Scale: Construction and validation. *Psychological Reports,* 5: 663–71.

Sim, J. P., & Romney, D. M. (1990). The relationship between a circumplex model of interpersonal behaviors and personality disorders. *Journal of Personality Disorders,* 4: 329–41.

Skodol, A. E. (1989). *Problems in differential diagnosis: From DSM-III to DSM-III-R in clinical practice.* New York: American Psychiatric Press.

Snow, R. E., Kyllonen, P. C., & Marshalek, B. (1984). The topography of ability and learning correlations. In R. J. Sternberg (Ed.), *Advances in the psychology of human intelligence.* Vol. 2: 47–103. Hillsdale, NJ: Erlbaum.

Sobel, M. E., & Bohrnstedt, G. W. (1985). Use of null models in evaluating the fit of covariance structure models. In N. B. Tuma (Ed.), *Sociological methodology 1985,* 152–178. San Francisco: Jossey Bass.

Spearman, C. (1904). "General intelligence" objectively determined and measured. *American Journal of Psychology,* 15: 201–93.

Spearman, C. (1927). *The abilities of man.* New York: Macmillan.

Spencer, H. (1855). *Principles of psychology.* London: Williams.

Srole, L. (1956). Anomie, authoritarianism, and prejudice. *American Journal of Sociology,* 62: 63–67.

Sternberg, R. J. (1977). *Intelligence, information processing, and analogical rea-*

soning: The componential analysis of human abilities. Hillsdale, NJ: Erlbaum.

Sternberg, R. J. (1980). Sketch of a componential subtheory of human intelligence. *Behavioral and Brain Sciences*, 3: 573–84.

Sternberg, R. J. (1983). Components of human intelligence, *Cognition*, 15: 1–48.

Sternberg, R. J. (1985). *Beyond IQ: A triarchic theory of human intelligence*. London: Cambridge University Press.

Sugarman, B. N. (1967). Involvement in youth culture, academic achievement and conformity in school: An empirical study of London schoolboys. *British Journal of Sociology*, 18: 151–64.

Sullivan, H. S. (1953). *The interpersonal theory of psychiatry*. New York: Norton.

Terman, L. L. (1919). *The intelligence of school children*. Boston: Houghton Mifflin.

Thurstone, L. L. (1938). *Primary mental abilities*. Chicago: University of Chicago Press.

Thurstone, L. L. (1947). *Multiple factor analysis*. Chicago: University of Chicago Press.

Triandis, H. C. (1971). *Attitude and attitude change*. New York: Wiley.

Tupes, E. C., & Christal, R. E. (1958). Recurrent personality factors based on trait ratings. *USAF ASD Technical Note*, No. 61–97.

Vernon, P. E. (1950). *The structure of human abilities*. New York: Wiley.

Wheaton, B., Muthén, B., Alwin, D. E., & Summers, G. F. (1977). Assessing reliability and stability in panel models. In D. Heise (Ed.), *Sociological methodology* 1977, 84–136. San Francisco: Jossey Bass.

Widiger, T. A., & Frances, A. (1985). The DSM-III personality disorders: Perspectives from psychology. *Archives of General Psychiatry*, 44: 615–62.

Widiger, T. A., Frances, A., Spitzer, R. L., & Williams, J. B. W. (1988). The DSM-III-R personality disorders: An overview. *American Journal of Psychiatry*, 145: 786–95.

Widiger, T. A., Trull, T. J., Hurt, S. W., Clarkin, J., & Frances, A. (1987). A multidimensional scaling of the DSM-III personality disorders. *Archives of General Psychiatry*, 44: 557–63.

Wiggins, J. S. (1982). Circumplex models of interpersonal behavior in clinical psychology. In P. C. Kendall & J. N. Butcher (Eds.), *Handbook of research methods in clinical psychology*, 183–221. New York: Wiley.

Wiggins, J. S., Phillips, N., & Trapnell, P. (1989). Circular reasoning about interpersonal behavior: Evidence concerning some untested assumptions underlying diagnostic classification. *Journal of Personality and Social Psychology*, 56: 296–305.

Wiggins, J. S., & Pincus, A. L. (1989). Conceptions of personality disorders and dimensions of personality. *Psychological Assessment: Journal of Consulting and Counseling Psychology*, 1: 305–16.

Wiggins, J. S., & Trapnell, P. D. (in press). Personality structure: The return of the Big Five. In S. R. Briggs, R. Hogan, & W. H. Jones (Eds.), *Handbook of personality psychology*. Orlando, FL: Academic Press.

Witkin, H. A., Lewis, H. B., Hertzman, M., Machover, K., Meissner, P. B., & Wapner, S. (1972). *Personality through perception: An experimental and clinical study*. Westport, CT: Greenwood.

Author Index

Subject Index

Abilities: defined, 17–18; factor model of, 18–20, 22; research problems, 18; and structural equation modeling, 18, 42–43, 115–16; theory of, as dynamic, 18, 43, 101–2; theory of, as hierarchies, 18, 22; theory of, as inherited, 18, 100; types of, 17. *See also* Intelligence

Achievement. *See* Abilities

Analysis of variance, 16

Attitudes, 1, 3, 100; common factor model of, 78, 81; defined, 75; measurement of, 79–80, 81; theory of, as dynamic, 81, 96; theory of, as hierarchies, 75–76, 80–81, 96

Attitudes, analysis of research data: quality-of-life study, 92–93, 96, 105; 16–19 Initiative study, 89–92; teenage smoking study, 81–83; United States Youth and Transition Study, 87–89, 96

Big Five dimensions of personality, 52–55, 69. *See also* Personality, theories of

Causality: causal relationships, 7–8, 37–38; and factor model, 42, 44, 110; limitations of interpretation, 9, 109–10; and path analysis, 26, 37, 110, 112; and regression, 9, 10, 15. *See also* Path analysis

Chi square. *See* Goodness-of-fit

Circulant matrix, 57

Circumplex model of interpersonal behavior, 55–57, 69, 97; and correla-

tion of variables, 57; defined, 27; history of, 55; and personality disorders, 59–61; and relation to hierarchical models, 50, 55–56; structural equation modeling of, 61–62. *See also* Attitudes; Intelligence; Personality

Cognitive behavioral therapy, 71, 72

Compulsive personality disorder, 61, 63, 65, 66

Computer programs: EQS, 61, 62; LISREL, 30, 31–32, 34–35, 39, 61–62, 67, 72, 83

Confirmatory factor analysis, 5, 32, 61

Construct validity, 4, 108–9

Convergent validity, 4, 6

Correlation matrix: and factor analysis technique, 5, 21, 29–30, 50, 94, 116; and personality traits, 2, 50; and structural equation modeling, 7, 13, 26–27, 57, 61–63, 66, 72

Cronbach's alpha coefficient, 108

Cross-sectional data, 114

Depression, 1, 72, 77, 92, 96, 104–5

Developmental disabilities, 101

Diagnostic and Statistical Manual of Mental Disorders (DSM-III-R), 58, 60, 61, 62, 63, 65, 66

Discriminant validity, 4, 6

Economic control, 91–92

Empirical examples. *See* Attitudes, analysis of research data; Personality, analysis of research data; Richmond Tests of Basic Skills

About the Authors

DAVID M. ROMNEY is Professor of Educational Psychology at the University of Calgary in Alberta, Canada. For the past twenty-two years he has taught full-time, and prior to that he practiced as a school psychologist and clinical psychologist.

JOHN M. BYNNER is Professor of Social Statistics and Director of the Social Statistics Research Unit at City University, London. He has also been the national coordinator of the U. K. Economic and Social Research Council 16–19 Initiative and is presently Director of the National Child Development Study and the 1970 British Cohort Study.

DATE DUE

GAYLORD			PRINTED IN U.S.A.